A Winter Apprentice

Earl's gloves and measuring tape,
a noon ritual, placed as mnemonic
for his first afternoon job.

A Winter Apprentice

John Holt Willey

Polar Bear & Company
An imprint of the
Solon Center for Research and Publishing
Solon, Maine

Polar Bear & Company™
Solon Center for Research and Publishing
PO Box 311, Solon, Maine 04979 U.S.A.
207.643.2795, polarbearandco.org, soloncenter.org

First print edition 2016
First printing April 2016
ISBN: 978-1-882190-45-4
Library of Congress Control Number: 2016937107

Back cover photo: author at home shop testing his just-completed Krenov-
style hand plane. Front cover photo of *Simba* courtesy of Penobscot Marine
Museum; the person on the bow is probably John Luke.

Author photo page 195 by Ramona du Houx. Aerial view of Paul Luke Yard
© 2013 Google. All other photos are from the author's collection.

Cover design by Ramona du Houx
Manufactured on durable acid-free paper in more than one country.

Fortune brings in some boats that are not steer'd.

Pisanio, *Cymbeline*, III, ii

—Shakespeare

Contents

Preface

Lovers of saltwater and sailing will find here stories from a unique shipyard in mid-coast Maine, toward the end of the 1970s. These are written by a lifelong boat-nut, from a journal I kept then. My story is of men and women daily making art in an environment awkward, hectic, loud, messy, painful, comic, and sad. I was exhausted much of the time, loved every minute of it, and might be there still if I had picked up my own work gloves one fine May morning. Someone else's had fingers longer than mine, and these pulled my hand into a machine.

Among the yard stories are a few from my own growing up, some from the lives of others, and a few specific to Maine and the nature of her people. My experience over time has confirmed my belief in the case I make here, that our only true knowledge, our bone-deep understanding of what we need as humans able to make a life and a world, is found in a life of apprenticeship or "apprenticehood," to use the old term evocative of a state of being from Shakespeare's *King Lear* and a passage from *Richard II*.

My closest friends are men and women who make things, sometimes for others, always for the joy in making. I dreamt of the yard again last night and waked happy. I wish you the same in your life.

I wanted some photographic record of what I knew from the start would be only a year or so in Paul's yard. Months passed before I understood that early letters to my father would in time become the journal and memoir you find here. I had no hint as to how long — once this began — how long it could perhaps take. Patience has always been something I envied in others but lacked myself. I wish now I'd been able to make a better photo record of my time in the yard.

Someone wrote long ago, "If you want to make God laugh, tell Him your plans." All I knew just then was that I meant to make a living for us by working wood, and any writing would have to be worked in around this. The notion firmed up following an exchange of letters with John

Gardner of National Fisherman and Mystic Seaport Museum, where
John curated and added to their small craft collections. John Gardner's
life and work by then had made him far more than a philosopher and
historian, who happened to build beautiful boats. I still treasure the
letters he found time to write me. They are the chief reason this book
exists. His first letter to me can be found in the appendix.

"Acknowledgement" is a word too thin to tell the debt I owe the
mentors and exemplars of my life—including all who try sometimes
for profit, also for fun—who make words and music dance, make
books, art, furniture, gardens, homes, tools— One makes a wood
casket so elegant its owner can keep his library in it until he occupies it
himself, until it and he once more become mutual atoms and memory.
The dearest of all teach what they themselves have learned, whenever
they find even a transient apprentice. All have taught me, mostly about
things I didn't know I didn't know.

I built two boats with my friend and schoolmate Carl at about age
seventeen. Neither of these involved aluminum, oak, ash, butternut,
mahogany, Thai teak, naval architects, my joiner foreman Earl Dodge,
or Paul Luke. Or Stanley Mitchell, still shaping wood for boats
when we met at Paul's. Stanley was the eldest in the yard that winter.
These gentlemen were individuals who held firm views on the art of
building boats (under construction and sometimes lifelong, the vessel
is a "boat," no matter the size), so my middle-age apprenticehood,
aided by an historic regional talent for brevity in speech, made for
early frustration in my learning process. I think, finally, that learning
boatbuilding is much like learning how to be married, with the added
benefit of a paycheck if you get it right. But once my mentors realized
I could "get it" by watching it done once and by asking as I watched,
things began to smooth out.

No coherent manuscript arrived until my fourth effort, about
1997–98. I kept writing because John Gardner thought highly of my
early chapters, and also because nearly all my own learning has been
through apprenticehood, a working for and with men and women who
knew what I wanted to know. My reading and experience over time
convinced me that this practice reaches into us in ways no schoolroom
ever could, and this persuaded me that maybe my story, of trying to
learn all I could in this one art, in this tiny, fine place, might help others
find confidence and the tools and experience they need to make their
own lives.

While still a young man, John Gardner became apprentice in a boatyard, found that he loved the work, and along with his studies in history and philosophy kept on building boats the rest of his life. I've met one or two who got to work with John at Mystic Seaport. They never got over it. He was a great teacher.

The time and events described here are unique—to me at least—in one aspect. I have yet to find another such journal written by a workman who labored by the clock, within such a yard, for a paycheck, at some work he or she came to love.

Artist and writer Jan Adkins loves the building of things, and has written about a PhD thesis he once read by a scholar who completed her degree by finding a traditional Japanese cabinetmaker, a *sashimonoshi*. Carol Ann Bartusiak Link traveled to Japan, moved in with Ojii-san's family and lived with them and their woodwork until she was confident she could deliver respectable woodwork and her thesis. Her book is *Japanese Cabinetmaking: A Dynamic System of Decisions and Interactions in a Technical Context* (University Microfilms International, Ann Arbor, MI). My copy is dog-eared with use.

The building at Paul's of floating, directionally stable vessels to take humans across deep water in some comfort and with some certainty of reaching the far side, this work in this place let me become, at age forty-five, the permanent apprentice I supposed I was at age twenty. I reached a point where I went to bed not knowing how to do the job I needed to do next morning and waked in the morning knowing, in many such events, the tools I would need, the sequence of work, and often the time I would need to complete the job. This had never happened to me before. It was humbling, exciting, mysterious to me, then and now, though it happens less often with more years behind me. Work, watch, listen, think, sleep, and some key turns. Others have described the same process to me.

Apprentice pay in those years was a life-support minimum. There was, somehow, always enough, and my blessed wife never complained, then or later. She could see I was learning both skills and art and that I was anxious to learn more. All in the yard were willing to share what they knew. That winter was, in learning, the happiest of my life. I hope these stories will reflect that, and hope my memoir will tell those living now who then worked beside me that I still treasure all they gave me and the kindness of their company while I was there.

Early readers have worried that the stories offer too little physical description and too little introduction to several of the crew. Where possible, I've tried to let the speech, behavior and work habits of my friends describe them. We all create our own composite friends every day, usually without noticing.

"There" was as much a state of mind as a spot on a map. These stories now and then offer hints of that state of mind. I dreamt of the yard, still do, though in most of my formal schooling I never dreamt at all.

Along with all who worked for Paul E. Luke in '78 and '79, I am in debt to writers who have left a book or story important to the kind of person I have been at different times in my life and so surely to the person I am. We are as often shaped by chance as by the predictable events, and this has surely been true of all my life.

I need to thank Chuck Lakin, Lauren Shaw, Nancy McGinnis, Matthew Murphy, Frank Southard, Cameron Weaver, and Hugh Roth, patient readers who offered thoughtful comment along the way, strengthening my experience with the gift of their own. Some of you have become part of the story, in the structure you gave it.

Among my teachers and readers are two who never met each other, but who taught English in different schools and many years apart, as both a discipline and an art form. If the result here makes you smile—or frown—then you can credit Dorothy Steinmeyer and, earlier, Miriam Kochakian.

About '96 or '97 a longtime friend said I should apply right away to the John Anson Kittredge Fund for a writing grant. I had never written a grant application and doubted the Fund would even respond to a query from an unpublished carpenter/apprentice. In due time, I received a personal note from a much-published historian and professor of history, reminding me gently that I had forgotten to say how much money I needed. The Kittredge Fund let me keep my truck, do some travel for research, and write long enough to produce at last a coherent, sequential draft. In essence, the Fund saved my bacon and this book, and its trustees are heroes to me.

Beyond all in the Faith and Patience Department is my wife Barbara, whose smile after fifty years of these and other adventures is still my most enduring reward.

Belgrade, Maine   J.H.W.
February, 2016

1

Barn Boats

Carl and I were seventeen that fall, best friends and bored senseless with the world—except for our interest in the work we did; seven days a week Carl in the dairy barn, where he was lead boy in caring for and milking about sixty head of Ayrshire cattle every night and morning, under Raymond Gifford's relaxed supervision. And myself in the horse barn, where I fed, watered, cleaned out, and daily fussed over nine huge animals, most of them older and all of them wiser than my callow self. And I daily cleaned and curried and drove Sandy, a tall, handsome buckskin, more used to answering Canadian French than to following my Maine Yankee efforts at horse-talk. Sandy and I took wagonloads of firewood, as needed, to the cottages on the boys' campus; on Saturday mornings we picked up the week's trash and hauled it far into the trees behind the barns, where (in those years) it gradually became landfill.

Carl and I lived and worked and went to school at Good Will Farm in Maine, and this was in the early 1950s. The same place is alive and thriving today, now called Good Will-Hinckley, still caring for other people's children in a rural riverside community of group-homes and schools. Founded 1889 by George W. Hinckley of Guilford Connecticut, it had grown to 3,500 acres by the 1950s, with more than fifty buildings and was home to about 140 boys and girls, age nine to twenty-one.

Nondenominational, the high school taught a college-prep curriculum, and the community gained a remarkably useful set of life skills. Boys and girls were segregated by "cottages" (huge farmhouses) and about a mile of highway. They attended only high school and chapel together and were ruled by all the best Victorian principles, applied on a basic middleclass Protestant ethic.

The school existed on charity, and while the kids worked before and after school, this was seen as our contribution to tuition. The cottage system worked because we all had chores, a dozen boys or girls in each house, supervised by an eagle-eyed matron/housemother. Mine baked at Thanksgiving a pie for every boy in her house, and while strict, cared for us all as if we were her own. Of course I did not understand this at the time. Much later, my own mother filled in the dots for me, right after I'd said something rude about Addie Kearney Lawler (matron) who, it seems, had twice prevented my summary expulsion.

College prep seldom includes coaching for the sudden independence of a student; at college I failed while some succeeded; my oldest living friend from that time became a respected civil engineer and helped keep Amtrak on the rails.

Carl and I arrived during World War II. Neither of us had a clue as to when the cows and horses had arrived, but we were sure they were better company than anyone else—except for Raymond Gifford in the dairy, Walter Price the farm manager, and a couple of cottage mates. Raymond and Walter had been mercifully patient in teaching me about draft animals and how to talk horse. And generally forgiving of my juvenile excesses, like dancing Sandy in circles when hitched to the pung, for the entertainment of Smith Cottage girls. Smith Cottage, on the girls residential campus, was closest of the girls' homes to the south campus, where the boys lived. A boy could reach it by a discreet woodland path, crossing Marten Stream at a shallow. Some did. I did, was careless, seen by a wide-awake cottage parent, and nearly got myself expelled.

Back to the pung, literally an eight-foot-long box on steel-and-wood runners. I had found that Sandy's steel-clad hooves would let him wheel in place on an icy surface, spinning the pung in circles, and that he liked to perform. So we did.

The little box flew in circles around the dancing horse, hurling ice chips in all directions from its runners. Sandy could always be sure of an apple or carrot after the exercise. And one of the girls was specially pretty, of course—now and then I made off with a donut or a kiss.

In late winter or early spring, Carl and I got to talking about boats. We decided to build one, and then two. The school was so brilliantly conceived it had its own sawmill, under which was a mountain of pine sawdust. We were not allowed to build our own boats, of course. This made the work far more worthwhile. It did not matter to us that the Kennebec River every spring was bank-to-bank full of pulp logs and not a safe navigable waterway. Our teachers and guardians saw the river as a hazard. We saw it as part of the world to be traveled.

We selected splendid pine planks of suitable length and not quite enough width. We walloped the boats together with "ten penny" (size 10d) nails and tar—stolen from the maintenance shop—working under the sawmill with hand-tools also liberated, temporarily every Saturday afternoon, from the same shop. The boats were about twelve feet long, of uncertain beam, but surely too narrow for their depth, and we meant to run them down the Marten Stream rapids, four rocky sets of whitewater, with the advent of ice-out. We nailed together the ugliest pine paddles you can imagine, rough and wide and ill-shaped, and used them when the time came.

We worked on the boats on Saturday afternoons because that was our only unsupervised time of the week. We would simply vanish, dig up the boats and planks, work like hell for four hours, bury the boats in sawdust, and run back to our cottages on Page Terrace to tuck into supper. I can still smell the pine, the tar and the cold nails—and the pitch we used to fill in the worst gaps, carefully gathered from blistery spruce on our way through the late-winter woods.

Just days after ice-out on the stream we got them done, and I kept Sandy in harness on a Saturday morning, when chores went quickly. Carl met me at the sawmill; we made sure no one else was in sight, and with the boats in the wagon, I put Sandy into the tote road to the oxbow on Marten Stream. At water's edge, we piled winter-killed brush on them and hurried back to the barns. I was late for dinner that day, but my housemother had a morning's turbulence on her mind, or my excuse was better than usual.

The following Saturday down the stream we went, somehow through all four rapids without spilling into the freezing water, somehow talking each other through in perfect ignorance of what we were doing.

Neither of us had ever heard of hypothermia, but in a moment of calm reflection a couple of weeks later, I found it in the dictionary— it was just after I'd helped Carl get dried out. We were to meet just below the first rapids on the stream, to manhandle the boats up past them and get another practice run. And Carl was missing. And his raw-wood boat and his paddle. I started to run down the shore path to the Kennebec River, but in less than a hundred yards I saw him, trudging toward me. On a cold blowing day, he had tried to cross the Kennebec, only to capsize in the acres of pulpwood offshore. Unable to reenter his boat, he somehow pulled it behind him to shore, fending off the logs and waste still being poured into the river in those years. A hundred feet or a hundred yards, he didn't know, but he was very pale and could hardly form words. God knows how he reached shore or walked so far. I knew just enough about cold to help him strip down to one layer and then to walk and finally run to his cottage, for dry clothing. He had set out with three layers on and must have been bone chilled by the time we met. The last I heard, Carl still has that boat. It rests on a stone fence in Readfield, on land his mother left him, still his home and harbor. I was careless; a spring freshet caught mine and took it downriver, probably crushing it in the logs.

Years later, visiting the school, I found Lawrence Easler, still chief of maintenance, working at the gym. In the war years and for long after, Lawrence looked after fifty-five large buildings, built wagons and boats, welded broken plow trucks and farm machinery, plumbed and electrified, ran a small municipal water system and repaired it when it broke, and on one memorable occasion borrowed me one day from school to move an old square grand piano from Belfast into the girls' campus library. We used his pickup truck, rope, plank, a handful of wedges, and Lawrence's perfect understanding of Archimedes. It was one of the more educational days of my young life. Lawrence was sturdy but not more than five foot eight or nine inches and could not be called muscular. I was plain skinny. Lawrence explained things to me as we went along, and I just followed instructions. We moved that piano without breathing hard once and set it in place without scratching its finish. By day's end, I finally understood that brain could ease brawn in most cases and that a little geometry was a truly beautiful thing.

Years later, idle by the gym in the warm sun, we'd chatted a few minutes when Lawrence asked, smiling, "John, whatever happened to those boats you and Carl built under the sawmill?"

My eyes wide, I told him about Carl's Readfield dry dock and my own carelessness and then asked, "When did you find out? And when you knew, why'd you let us keep on? If Norman Hinckley'd known, I'd still be scrubbing floors here!"

My surprise pleased Lawrence, "Well, I missed a handsaw one

Saturday. And then some tar from a can I thought was full. And anyone building something had to get wood for it. So I scouted a little and then saw some tracks under the sawmill and found the boats. After a little while, I knew who it was. You came back for some more tar!" He grinned again.

I was goggle-eyed: "And you never told."

"Didn't seem to be any reason to. The boats were small, but they were pretty sturdy and looked like they'd keep you from drowning. That was the only thing concerned me. So I'd go check on them after you and Carl were done."

"Every time?"

"Well, yes . . ."

Every week, when the boys were in Sunday school far from the barns and mill, Lawrence would patiently dig up the boats, check them over, and once more cover them with sawdust. And Carl and I never knew.

"They were small boats, so you weren't planning to go very far with them. And I never saw boats built with so few tools, so I got curious. As I remember, you didn't trouble too much with paint."

"No," I smiled, "a quick coat on the outside was all. We were kind of in a hurry—"

"But they worked all right," he said, "even with those paddles. Those were pretty rough, I thought."

"Oh, they were rough all right."

So Lawrence was pleased with his surprise and that he had figured right. And I was pleased that this remarkable man had broken the rules for us and taken on himself extra work to make sure our work was right and that we were, in fact, responsible enough to do some growing up on our own. It was the first time in my life I knew anyone allowed me that.

2

Down the Line

My home village looked less comforting than I remembered.
Myself burnt out from what one doctor supposed out loud
might be an excess of empathy, I'd closed up my office in San Francisco
in 1975 and with wife Barbara, one pet cat, and bits of our lives in
a tiny U-Haul, started east for home. In sixteen years as a reporter
and private investigator, I had not learned how to separate from my
self the suffering of my clients and had to take time to learn the art.
We drove first to Iowa and Barbara's people. I fished farm ponds and
wrote a godawful detective novel, from which I was rescued in the
nick of time by an agent willing to actually read a manuscript for a
modest sum. Barbara had hip replacements at Mayo Clinic, Rochester,
a pleasant city surrounded by too few trout.

We finally were restored enough to travel east once more, though
Barbara was nervous about living among Yankees in far-off Maine.
The legend of standoffish bluenoses in the deep woods is just that, but
the legend is alive and well in Iowa AND California.

At the littlest house on Spring Street, at home, my mother was wel-
coming despite having had only vacation and overnight visitors for the
time between my last summer visit following high school and our arrival
in a July swimming with heat—and worrisome with few jobs available.

In the year 1977 our president was James Earl Carter, who liked to
be called Jimmy. At home the one grocery and the house hand built by
the oldest voter in the village were painted, but the rest of Main Street
looked unloved. Uppers and downers were traded in daylight at its one
major intersection, while its one constable was somewhere else, for
equally pressing reasons.

It didn't take long to learn that the village of Home, still occupied by less than three thousand souls, put a concerned look in the eye of employers two counties distant. The local newspapers identified people arrested that week, sometimes listing their home town, and this did make a difference to employers. Industry in Home was a wood-frame woolen mill, where relentless looms clacked twenty-four hours every day. Today the mill is razed; a pretty town park now lives beside the Sebasticook River, which once turned a sawmill owned by my grandfather Holt, years before he learned the joys of running a general store.

I got my fishing license signed by the town clerk, son of the town clerk who attested Arthur Shaw's statement as attending doctor, on the certificate Shaw signed as to my live birth. This at least was positive, as was a visit with my mother's father. Ancestor worship is closer to home than we might think; in Maine the family farmstead can have dry rot in the roof and two feet of water in the cellar as long as Grampa's cemetery grass is cut and the stone stands true. At least it can look that way. The truth is often something else entirely—a little old lady with starched hair, frock and spine, often the last of her name, surviving on gumption and a tiny garden plot, keeping the geography of her future neat with a pair of garden shears. Her smile denies the existence of crippling arthritis, and if you keep both eyes open, you learn she's helping a couple of families less fortunate than herself.

Grandfather, who made his life and a family here, helping prod the place toward a reasonable prosperity in another bad time, was in no mood for conversation. The burying ground looked fine and trim, as ever. The prospect toward the town's few employers stopped at $2.75 an hour, rock bottom at that time, even for Maine.

I put my fishing gear in the car and without realizing it began my regional Market Research Program, in between streamside meditations. At a plant to the north, bustling with orders for a national furniture retailer, the machinery gleamed and spun, while folks inserted wood at one end of each cycle and extracted it at the other, milled with micrometer neatness and ready for the next machine. "Incentive system" was their term for the quota that kept rising as an employee got more efficient at his or her job. Union shop and a sharp smell of union unrest in the air—you look at folks long enough, and you can catch the sense of their thought or opinion. The only smile I saw was in the personnel office, which had yet to become the Human Resources Department.

Three towns off was a small factory turning out windows set in furniture-grade teak and mahogany, a chance for experience with exotic woods, and the machined results wanted a human hand afterward. At the start of my second week in Vassalboro, I was sent without comment to work at the finishing tables, alongside the three oldest hands. They had a good supply of bodies for the work, so there was no mention of a raise in pay. They had boys lined up on the street, so to speak, waiting.

This experience got me out of the house and taught me to look at machinery with care. Modern machines have protective guards, some of which actually preserve life and limb. Some just prevent quick neat work.

A big shaper at mid floor spent several hours a week finger-jointing teak and mahogany short lengths into useful stock. Tuned up properly, this thing set up a sub-audible standing wave that lined us up at the men's room, and its master (nope, not me) was never, never constipated. A four-sider is a machine capable of milling finished shapes into four sides at once on most sizes of prepared stock. When the four-sider ran at the same time as we were sanding at the finishing tables, we tended to run out of dust-masks and then out of breath. OSHA (the federal Occupational Safety and Health Administration) was a possibility but not a presence. Some of the machinery was born soon after James Watt, beautiful with cast-iron curlicues and furbelows, traces of shining black and gold if I rubbed away the years of grease and wood dust. If it works, or has worked, or might be coaxed into working, Maine tends to keep it and try to make money with it until change is forced.

I have to inject a priceless line from *Brittanica* here: "Apprenticeship declined as the Industrial Revolution progressed during the 18th century, but attempts were yet made to maintain traditional standards. In 1756 the city guilds in Glasgow refused to recognize the inventor James Watt because he had not served his full term as an apprentice . . ."

And we still look at far too much work of every kind without ever seeing the maker or perceiving his/her potential.

I noticed enough unguarded machinery to change my mind about safety and left to try some solo work.

It was a long winter. At home snow rose twice to the windowsills, sparrows and chickadees studying us inside my mother's kitchen—face to face, solemn as we looking back. I divided my time between a jury-rigged shop in Mother's soggy cellar, reading every James Krenov book

I could find, and pursuing furniture vendors for anything they could tell me. James Krenov at mid century was a respected independent cabinetmaker, working in Sweden. He taught first by personal example, then by writing, and later more formally at College of the Redwoods in northern California. His books and his work are prized I think for the depth, breadth and quality of the vision pursued in both. Krenov lived by a deceptively simple philosophy, was a role model to many, and an inspiring writer. Look him up, he's worth your time.

*   *   *

"A trestle table is a trestle table," said the lady in her coastal shop.

I continued the pursuit of vendors. "Hobby horses—like that one," said a man pointing to a cheerful little horse with its wheels set on spindles far too thin for safety. I moved along.

"I have to keep the floor full," a manager said, frowning, "or folks think we can't fill orders. Can you make me thirty beds like that?" Not with one radial-arm saw and hope, I couldn't. But how wonderful to be thought capable, maybe even prosperous.

"Yeah, say, I c'd sell a hundrid gahden ladies 'f you bring 'em by Friday week." These lawn ornaments sell steadily all summer long and at Christmastime. But my head was in furniture and wouldn't come out.

A thoughtful architect, an older man, who'd survived his own ruins young, had time to talk. "Maine is a wry neck of the woods," he said. "These are make-do people, the people here, now survivors in a place many have used up and left. The big business is gone or going, government providing more and more money but no work." And he guessed a third of the state was getting some form of assistance. Not much left over, anytime.

His theory neglected the forest-products industry, as well as the biggest commercial shipyard on the northeast coast, and a recent publication suggesting there were more millionaires per capita resident in Maine than in other states, but in essence he was right. The big mills, hiring the single-skill blue collar, had left or were leaving. And we both knew men and women working two full-shift jobs just to keep the family afloat.

He'd nearly gone under himself, until he found a gap in small-factory design that wanted filling. He was beginning to do better, as employers from away began to discover there was still a pool of skill and talent north of Kittery. He thought I might make a living: "You'd," pointing at me, "do fine in New York or Boston, if transport costs don't eat you up."

He was more than kind; he was helpful and pulled me a little closer to the border of The World As It Is. But if you have a gutful of cities and your experience inclines you to mine the Piscataqua and uproot Kittery Bridge, you may be hard of hearing. I was.

That winter was painfully long, and the following spring and summer gave little relief. I managed to build a carving bench for Barbara and a big joiner's bench on the German pattern. My joiner's bench would not go up the skinny cellar stairs, but with its shoulder vise hinged and its leg frames off, it could be got out a skinny basement window.

As a sort of self-test of skills, I hand planed the rock-maple bench top to useful flatness. By the time I finished, my plane blades were easier to sharpen and adjust, and my appreciation for the agony carved into all those medieval saints and sinners on old German altarbacks was deep and comprehensive: my fingers were routinely cut and cramped from gripping bare blades on the honing stones; one thumb was lame from the plane locking up midway on one pass with all my upper-body weight behind it, and my shoulders at the end of the day felt as if they'd been leaning on a jackhammer all week.

I was more humble about my skills and had far more admiration for all those shadowy figures out of Colonial times, working with limited tools on hard, hard woods. The Dominy family in East Hampton, New York, like all who came before and after, earned their daily bread. Diversification was their norm; the Dominys would make you six chairs, harden your gun hammer, mend rakes, hang a grindstone, survey your land, make and fit your window sash, mend your bellows, get your hay into the barn, and put you to rest in pine or fine mahogany (Aldren A. Watson, *Country Furniture*). Gradually, very gradually, the planes stayed sharp longer; maple and oak and other woods cut more readily; James Krenov's words made more sense as they worked through my hands and fingers; the perfume of cherry and walnut sawn or planed with sharp-edged tools made more effort possible, and the neighbors began to ask me to make small pieces, a tabletop, a drawer to replace one lost in moving.

The candle lighting most of that year caught fire while I was trudging through a specially miserable time of try-it-and-see. Krenov came to Boston to speak, invited by a merchant selling woodworking tools. Barbara and I drove to Boston and watched him hold spellbound an auditorium stiff with calluses and broken fingernails for most of three hours. When I remember there are as many methods of working wood as there are woodworkers, I'm still amazed at that day. The sponsor had to change the venue in haste three times that morning to accommodate a crowd of more than five hundred; some of them had arrived overnight from Florida, Detroit, and other unsung hotbeds of ancient craft.

The man's voice shook as he began; he said he was more used to a handful of men and women gathered around a dusty bench and sketches traced on scrap wood. At the end of two rounds of slides and the hours of his quiet voice describing ways of looking at things, we all stood up and applauded long and loud. As his books don't preach, neither does Krenov. I think he is more a philosopher who lives in his wood and his vision than a woodworker who is trying to teach a specific set of skills. I should add that many wives and girlfriends came with their men. Man or woman, few took time out for a pit-stop while he spoke.

The one thing he asked of us was that we try for the highest in quality, inside and out, in all work we might do. Many have.

James Krenov died at age 88, teaching at College of the Redwoods on the Mendocino coast. One of the better places on this planet to pursue a degree of grace. His books will live as long as mankind will hunt for an ethical life and for reason to do good work. Along with his own work, he brought forth a generation of apprentices.

On a late July expedition, hot and tired from fighting traffic on the Maine coast, I heard one vendor's plea, "Say, now, you travel a lot, can you find me some antiques?"

By 1978 I was forty-five, graying, long since had been made to feel too old in a labor market set on employing the young, the dyed, and the fashionable. I went back to the car and started for Home. By the time I arrived it was so dark that Main Street looked good. This apparition sent me to my dwindling supply of Goodness and Mercy—prized local label, lethal in excess—and next morning, with small confidence but a larger compass, back to the coast for a different purpose.

*   *   *

"Now that's pretty good," said the man in the office, looking up from the photo album, "but our contracts this year are all steelwork. Can you weld?"

I tried not to look sadly at him or at the sparkling river under his windows at South Bristol. "No, sorry," I said, "never done metalwork before."

He looked down again at the book. I mouthed a silent yes, in case he was scraping local talent deep enough to teach a new man to weld plate. He leafed back to a picture of the big maple workbench, a second long look.

In the little room it was hot, and the rank smell of rockweed thick. The wall clock ticked more life out of us standing sweating in the quiet. In the cluster of big, shadowy caves attached to the far wall, a ship-saw started, then stopped. Much later, remembering, I knew the workman forgot to draw part of his cutline curve. With a long breath, the owner pulled his eyes back to me, asking, "You been to Paul Luke?"

"No," but a question or two might save miles, "what's he build?"

In that climate it took about two minutes to copy the brief speech. "Yachts, mostly . . . guess his hulls're, uh, steel, aluminum, dunno, really. But there's an awful lot of finish. You oughta see him."

"Where is he?"

"Oh, down the line, Boothbay. East Boothbay, I think. And there's a lot more builders round there, besides." He pondered. "I'd see 'em all, 'f I was you."

Down the line. A lot more. Over. Beyond. The magic words. I pried a little more geography out of this kind man and headed north toward U. S. Route 1. Early afternoon, but still no breeze. A foraging seagull can wing his way from South Bristol to Boothbay Harbor in minutes, a beeline flight of three and a half miles. A driver, though, has to drive up and down long points of glacier-carved rock now topped (on the Boothbay Peninsula) by a mixed temperate forest and about five thousand year-round residents. The road from Bristol to Boothbay is about twenty-five miles and in summer made hazardous by a further forty-five thousand souls who with good reason see the point and its several deepwater yacht ports as a grand place to vacation and recreate. The road is improved at the middle of your trip by inclusion of Route 1, which in summer can creep its two lanes of traffic through our scenic villages at the speed of septic sludge, enriching the very air for any driver not cocooned in air conditioning.

I used the leisurely drive to meditate again on what to say to potential employers. Qualifications: a lifetime love of boats, a modest set of hand-tool skills, eighteen months making and repairing furniture for neighbors, a few photos of work done. A willingness to learn. Years enough to distinguish between a showy surface and a thorough quality. Broke.

Deficits: no boatbuilding experience, little time working with big power tools, exactly two months of my life spent working inside factories building industrial products, years of work that had nothing to do with boats or men who built them. Too old? And broke. And hungry. Near the Harbor shopping area I stopped for coffee and a sandwich. Pale women in exotic sunglasses and all known shapes and shades of Bermuda shorts strolled by, studying prices and New England village architecture, the occasional cockapoo pissing on a storefront.

I listed builders at a pay phone and set out. Most of the old names remembered from lobster feed treks as a boy with my mother were gone, so imagined names will do here. Titanic Oceanic had gone bust with a steel trawler half done, a white and final paper taped to the shed door. Epoxy & Company was going well, but so was my allergy. Archetype & Sons. It was noon and the boss gone, but the young office girl sounded like Dame Experience, so I listened. She named the commercial yards and the yacht yards close by, gave me a compact lesson in the relative amounts of woodwork in each, and "You stick to the yacht yards"; she smiled, looking through the book of photos, "You'll get work. Must be one of 'em needs a joiner. You tried Paul Luke yet?"

"No," I was trying to see the closer yards first. The price at the pump was rising again, the transmission making an interesting noise.

More overs and beyonds, "East Boothbay, through the village, and watch on your right in a mile or so."

On the way I looked in at Glass, Mastick & Sanders; Grand, Puritan & Company; John Rampage; and Shrewd & Rowdy. At the last, they were dickering for a hundred-footer in wood, but "He ain't signed yet and may not." He looked up at me again, "Say, where you gonna live 'f you get on 'th someone? I doubt they's a house empty on the point this yeah. Summuh folks'll give two hundred a week f'r a fowah holah." He grinned. Then he suggested a couple of rentals, so I kept on.

I bumbled past it twice, shoved along by urgent vacationers. For this coast, the heat was unreal; I had all the windows down and was

Paul E. Luke boatyard on Linekin Bay, Maine.

stifling. Through the trees a cluster of sheds by the water—no sign, not a boat in sight. While I stopped for traffic to clear, the breeze finally came, summer-soft, then thick brawn, semen-salt-smelling, the body odor of the North Atlantic ocean.

Toward one end of a low shed front, an open door let me into a supply-and-shipping room. Nobody around, no sound but the breeze riffling packing slips. Racks of winches, hatches and heads, seagoing infernals electric and electronic, propellers, shafting, anchors, one or two stoves, vent hoods, turnbuckles, blocks, near two miles of yacht nylon at a price that would make a banker blanch. A scrunched cigarette butt almost under one bench. I once did work that required looking for scrunched butts and other debris and couldn't—can't—seem to break the habit. "But that was in another country, and besides, the wench is dead." Rowdy young, dead young, Marlowe; I leave it be.

It dawned on me, standing neck deep in portable wealth, that no bell or buzzer waked any occupant to an incoming stranger. Surprising, I thought, when already half the factories in California kept a guard at the gate; I wondered if only in Maine is paranoia more likely between neighbors than between strangers. Smelling teak dust over diesel, I followed my nose. A small metal *greech* spoke underfoot, a non-human, non-machine sound; the teak odor pulled me on.

The far door led to a cubicle stiff with wire, hastily marked small boxes, and a floor heavy with big marine batteries. Turning beyond them, I stumbled into church.

For most a church is a structure set aside for common or group worship. For me a church is any place careful, thoughtful, and life-affirming work is done. Among such workplaces, a boat- or shipyard has to be both life-affirming and life-preserving, and at its heart is the joiner shop, the holy of holies.

It had that look, and I suppose for me it always will: rows of big, dusty chests, thick-lidded, ranged under long benches at each wall, practical pews marching up the nave toward a bandsaw chancel, skylighted, dense with incense; heaps of sawdust, windrows of curling plane shavings, racks of bronze and stainless screws and bolts. A glue-frame, a set of human-size bench and power tools, shapes softer under dusty skylights; saw, shaper, thickness planer under the quiet authority of the towering bandsaw, waiting. A railed gulf in mid floor dropped to the timber stacks and a radial-arm saw—a crypt, with sculpture, sleeping, waiting transfiguration. The shadowy room lacked one thing: a hand-shaped hand plane, one flank cut bold with INRI, adrift on one of the altars. My eye made one and then lost it, tripping over a Bailey's patent jack plane on the near bench, above the sturdiest, least-dusty chest. No sound, nobody in sight.

I wanted to work here.

Turning yet again, I found another doorway on the shadow side of the wire room. A friend warned me, in an uncertain place one time, that doors have far more than hinges and latches attached to them, and mirrors more than reflection. "Be sure you want to step through," she said, "or that you have to look. Because you may be a long time coming back." I was very young then and knew a great deal and just smiled at her. Now I know a great deal less, but I've learned to listen to my friends.

A drunken, very logical walkway led through more echoing sheds to a four-way junction. Following the John Theory of Junctions, I took the emptiest passage. Something less than math supports my theory, but it will usually take you to the front office, and it did this time. Nobody home.

A fine set of half-models on the walls, papers strewn across several desks, half-acre of plant, tools and stock open, vacant, void of workmen on a workday. No office help. I began to shift feet like

a nervous schoolboy. I'd seen a boss come right out of his tree on
finding a stranger with no escort deep in his preserve. This was getting
eerie. A familiar sound, a big lathe hummed to life beyond the far wall.
I took a deep breath and another wrong turn before finding it, "Paul
Luke here?"

The machine shop was far bigger inside than out. "Nope!" yelled
a distant figure at the spinning lathe, waving "round in the big shed!"
Two more wraiths glanced up, while a ghost whizzed across the
junction behind me. I let the metal door thud shut and trudged out
into the big shed. From behind and below a giant hydraulic press, I
could see two men standing on an oddly exotic bridge over a further
gulf to a—well, I guessed, maybe a million or so dollars in gleaming
aluminum, a yacht cradled high above the concrete. My jaw was still
dropping as I stepped onto the jangling gangway and the near set of
shoulders, dark and heavy, spun on me with a barked "Yes!"

3

Apprentice Work (Yacht Work!)

The man apparently heard something useful before my voice quit, but I was standing staring at a photograph—a face out of context, out of place, out of time, when I heard, "Wal, come up t' the office." The voice warmed up, "Let's get outta this noise."

Startled, I hurried to follow him off the gangway, so off balance from the gulf below and the gap in memory that I kept a hand on each railing. It was the voice, I finally knew, spinning back at me before he'd turned to face me. Now harsh, now nasal, almost plaintive at times, most often a drawling, Downeast plainchant, it should have cracked authority like a field gun; for an instant there in the shed, in mid air, Rameses II glared at me, flesh come to shocking life, commanding, imperial, absolute. If those eyes found a thing worth doing, they would spend their owner's life and wealth seeing that thing done.

Of average height and solid build, perhaps only weight of shoulder would pick him from a crowd, that or his walk, a pace with little roll to it, however much time he spent on salt water. It was more a steady, quiet advance with power in it, always in balance, focused like a gymnast about to spring, like a warrior at practice in kendo. In marine painting from the eighteenth and nineteenth centuries, you can find sometimes a handsome small oil of a cutter or dispatch boat ranging to windward of a suggested fleet, ahead, alert, vigilant. The dark-blue shoulders reached the office and turned; I was transfixed again, while Paul examined his visitor: "Lookin' for work, y' say," he drawled, glancing at my hands. However odd it sounds in this context, I have yet to meet a tailored captain of industry so impressively present as this middle-aged man in his daily dark-blue work clothing and sturdy blunt shoes. The eyes inspected further, while I tried to make useful noise and describe past jobs.

Mesmerized, I'd clean forgot the voice when it lashed out again, "You WHAT?"

The textbook employment interview has no footnote help for those afflicted with hoof-in-mouth disease. I'd had the first seizure of many that would curse our dealings from that day on: "Ah . . . I was an investigator—tort claims, mostly—for some law firms in San Francisco 'til we moved," I gulped, and shut up.

What I'd said was evidently worse than a fart in church. Paul gave me a smoldering stare and time to understand more than I wanted to know about explosive silence, before he asked, "Ever work for Raptor, Entrales & Corvidy out there?"

"N-no. I know the name, corporation law, I think. I only worked for the tort- and criminal-law men." My hair was beginning to singe, "Why?" I ventured. I knew some unpopular lawyers but had never heard an entire firm dissolved in acid before. Somehow Montgomery Street had gouged a hole in this Downeast granite.

The fierce eyes dropped. He'd had some trouble, he said. Over money—and a racing hull . . . It couldn't have been my hair, I decided, with sweat running down my neck. Bits of the story came to me months later: it hinged on the intrinsics of a racing hull, a form more important to one species of psychopath than the shape of his beddable mistress. The law firm had cost the yard, at a bad time.

"Y'd be willing to move here, y' say?"

"Yes—soon's we can find a place."

"Well . . ." he picked up my too-thin photo album, then turned back to me as he closed it, "y' want to see the bo't?" He smiled slightly. We patrolled out to the big shed again, this time moving fast enough so I learned Rule One: he wanted no workman who ambled. For his purposes, Paul had methods efficient as those of any analyst. Some yards I'd seen on the other coast might have put three pretty hulls on San Francisco Bay for the cost of this gleaming whale of a cruising hull, a ketch, I guessed, still months from completion. It would take a tall stick and a power of wind to drive her, but she looked like nine knots sitting in her cradle.

" 'Bout sixty-five foot," Paul said, "biggest we've done, so fah." To my novice eye, she was blinding—an acre of aluminum curves, keel to deckhouse top—and through her main-cabin ports, wood. Lots and lots of beautiful wood, more butternut than I knew existed.

Across the gangway at a fair trot, I finally could see and hear work in progress, all of it below decks, at the moment remarkably quiet except for a modest mumble in the doghouse (raised-roof cabin forward of the vessel's cockpit). I had a glimpse of a woman's arm waving in the neat sweeps required by a varnish brush, while two young male voices chanted numbers back and forth. Wondering if they had a private system for classifying visitors, I finally saw they were testing a multithrow switch, working from a deckhouse control board complex enough to hold its owner's attention when it came time for him to push buttons.

Trying to see it all at once, of course I could see only bits and pieces, glimpses; corrugated cardboard and rough plywood protected deck surfaces and occasional spans of naked framing; the doghouse (deckhouse) interior was best butternut everywhere. Every surface melted easily from flat to curve; every projection was softened to ease eye and careless elbow. An older gent, apparently the senior softener, was installing an overhead grab rail with energy uncommon in men younger than myself. While most of my sailing had been in yachts built to a tight budget, I'd spent half my boyhood with my dry-land nose in books and magazines rich in photos of the handsome joinery found in gold-platers from the '20s and '30s. Herreshoff, Trumpy, Nevins, John Alden, Starling Burgess, the names still tumble through my head, famous names of American yacht building in that time.

A sizeable chunk of life spent on non-boat work had persuaded me that the fine joiner work came to a halt with World War II, but in a cabin of almost solid brightwork, every inch here was in proportion to the space and its use and furnishing. The girl, the older gent, and the only electrician I could see nodded and smiled. It must have been plain I couldn't wait to get at it—this was as right as any yachtwork I'd ever see. Full of enthusiasm and other unbalancing emotions, I turned to Paul and blurted, "I can do that!"

Paul smiled slightly, and a snort erupted from underfoot. The snorter was out of sight, toiling deep in the engine room, but there was no doubting his target: I was the snortee. One smile broadened, two disappeared, and my prospective employer looked reflective. I may not have been calibrating snorts too well. Paul nodded, and we patrolled back to his office.

Without putting a desk between us, he eyed me up and down—
little beef and no brawn—then explained carefully and clearly in non-
Yankee, taking his time about it, that his whole business was hard work,
that I'd had a look only at the easy part, a glance, really, no more. He
studied something beyond my view for a moment, something beyond
the outer door, then turned back to me, drawling, "And I'm said t' be
a hahd man t' work foah."

"I'll manage," I said.

He was, and I did. We both did. We managed to learn a little about
each other; we managed to misconstrue, each of us, much of what the
other said and did; we managed occasionally to ignore each other; we
managed a few times to amuse and amaze the rest of the shop, and
a couple of ninety-decibel managings sent half the shop diving for
cover. We managed to smile at each other and say good morning, and
mean it. We managed to confuse me and upset and anger each other.
I never, on any day I worked for Paul, saw him confused. Somewhere
in there, we managed to engrave on odd bits of my anatomy a useful
amount of practical shipbuilding and with that a better understanding
of the bodies and brains it takes to do it. Do it so you can be proud
of it. We managed wonderfully well for thirty-six weeks, and then we
managed to shake hands once more.

Considering that my life had been trauma, tragedy, lawyers and
reluctant witnesses, and that Paul's life was (I began to see) the creation
of workmen and the building of stunning sea boats, I guess we
managed pretty well. He managed better than I did, though: Paul knew
how to be angry and patient at the same time, so he had more than
enough energy to manage a new hand into shape, structure, dimension
and balance. I finally came to think his boats were an excuse to build
something else.

We dickered a few minutes. Nervous, I repeated myself: I'd done
small repairs and sailed and read a great deal about boatbuilding but
had never built yachts or even worked steadily on one. This didn't seem
to worry him, "How much d'you think you're worth?" He grumbled
over a wage I knew I could live on for at least a few months, $3.50 an
hour (this was summer 1978), and said, "I think you're overchargin' f'r
your inexperience" and shook hands on it. I was to come as soon as I'd
found a summer apartment. I looked at the roadside again on my way
out: no sign identifying Paul E. Luke anywhere.

I don't really remember the drive home or the way the river looked in the late, red sun. I finally had something in my hands, work I had always wanted should the chance come. It looked like someone thought I was a joiner, though I was ignorant of most joints not part of a household or barroom. Somebody thought I could help build big, graceful yachts and was ready to back his notion with cash, always a useful if transient thing to have in hand. It looked like a lot of things, driving home, and Barbara was happy about it for both of us when I told her. It didn't look like I was crazy as a bug in bourbon, and it most of all didn't look like I'd stepped through one of that friend's doors from so long ago.

4

Apprenticehood

My interview with Paul fresh in mind, this seems the place to record a further, wholly unexpected "meeting" soon after, very much linked to this my first really new job in eighteen years.

We moved into a Boothbay apartment (former sea captain's house) that would be our winter quarters, in time to let me begin work about 1 August. Only a few weeks into my new job, while digesting Barbara's fine dinner, idly leafing through my beloved *Shakespeare, The Complete Works*, Cambridge Edition Text, as Edited by William Aldis Wright, Including the Temple Notes, Illustrated by Rockwell Kent, with a Preface by Christopher Morley, 1936—I crashed head first into King Lear.

My life has had a truly modest share of smooth transitions, and I knew on that idle evening, when I came across the astonishing lines that open Scene IV in Act I of *Lear*, that my new job was not going to be one of them. An employment interview if ever I saw one, the Earl of Kent's Act I exchange with his increasingly mad king has stuck with me ever since. To see why, you first have to meet Miss Crosby, who is the sole reason I've trucked my single-volume *Complete Shakespeare* everywhere for more than half my life—and clear to the granite-ledge edge of Maine.

Miss Crosby was tall, angular, middle-aged, homely and bespectacled, but she *sang* into our farm-bred, school-kid heads the Bard's words—lines from *As You Like It*, ideas finally comprehended by the thirty boys and girls listening to her and the steam radiators along the wall, in the sleepy afternoon sunlight at Good Will Home's Averill High School. I can't speak for the other kids, their memories, but her feelings about that one play, *As You Like It*, came across as music. Since her usual classroom tone was one of patient exasperation, her voice in reading lines from *As You Like It* was by itself as remarkable to our ears as the poetry she chose to read.

Years after school and U.S. Marine Corps service, I found my cherished copy in 1962—Holmes Book Company, Third St. at Market in San Francisco—and somehow have kept it safe ever since, talisman of secret boatbuilding days and my boyhood discovery of the power of books. In SF I would fall into an armchair after a bad day spent searching for witnesses at various accident scenes and become a very different detective with Shakespeare.

At last safely back in Maine, I found Miss Crosby, age ninety, living with her niece's family, clearly able to remember me and to recite lines—"books in the running brooks, sermons in stones"—from *As You Like It*, the single play in our aging textbooks. She was pleased I remembered. We had tea and chatted a while. In a few weeks she was gone. Her thoughtful niece remembered her visitor and called me.

What yanked me out of my Boothbay armchair to march around the living room reading were the opening lines of Act I, Scene IV, in *King Lear*—the second interview between the Earl of Kent (this time in disguise and clean-shaven) and Lear—plain and vivid, an employment interview, short, spiky, good-humored, and vital to the later action. Lear's wits are going but not his appetite: his mind at the moment is on dinner.

For those not acquainted with the play, please know I had somehow never before read it nor seen the play on stage or screen; we teens had been thought too tender to absorb such profound matters, and that evening I opened the book at random.

Though I was unprepared by the opening three scenes, the lines that struck me with so much force still need introducing here. Lear's aging wits are so distressed he has given his kingdom to greedy (to say the least) daughters Goneril and Regan and to their husbands, the dukes of Albany and Cornwall. In the same court audience, he has disinherited and banished Cordelia, his youngest daughter, who truly loves him—because she will not make public declaration of her feelings, despite knowing her sisters care nothing for Lear and want only their father's wealth and power. When the Earl of Kent speaks up on Cordelia's behalf, Lear banishes him as well.

Visiting (with due entourage) the castle of daughter Goneril and her husband, Lear has exhausted his welcome to the point where his hosts are ready to chuck him out.

Opening Scene IV, Kent has shaved off his abundant beard and managed to disguise himself. He is determined to find some way to protect the king he truly loves. Lear arrives in hall, hunting dinner and his fool. The old man, if you read rather than listen to the play, proceeds to hold an interview that an employer today could use to test the wits of any nervous prospect. And as a very recent nervous prospect, I had good reason to study the Earl's replies in context of my own. AND to wonder again what part of my interview Paul liked well enough to ignore my lack of experience and practical knowledge in the building of a good, sound, sea-kindly boat.

Now, many years later, I've been able to watch two prized versions of *King Lear*, one with Sir Lawrence Olivier and, much earlier (black and white!), Orson Welles, both done for TV. And I discovered something the words by themselves don't transmit. More about that after you have the words, the words Will Shakespeare left us.

[Enter Kent, in disguise.]

KENT
If but as well I other accents borrow
That can my speech diffuse, my good intent
May carry through itself to that full issue
For which I razed my likeness. Now, banished Kent,
If thou canst serve where thou dost stand condemned,
So may it come thy master whom thou lov'st
Shall find thee full of labors.

[Horns within. Enter Lear, knights and attendants.]

LEAR
Let me not stay a jot for dinner; go get it ready.
[Exit an attendant.]
How now, what art thou?

KENT
A man, sir.

LEAR
What dost thou profess? What wouldst thou with us?

KENT
I do profess to be no less than I seem; to serve him truly that will put me in trust; to love him that is honest; to converse with him that is wise and says little; to fear judgment; to fight when I cannot choose, and to eat no fish.

LEAR
What art thou?

KENT
A very honest-hearted fellow, and as poor as the king.

LEAR
If thou be as poor for a subject as he is for a king, thou art poor enough. What wouldst thou?

KENT
Service.

LEAR
Who wouldst thou serve?

KENT
You.

LEAR
Dost thou know me, fellow?

KENT
No, sir; but you have that in your countenance which I would fain call master.

LEAR
What's that?

KENT
Authority.

LEAR
What services canst thou do?

KENT
I can keep honest counsel, ride, run, mar a curious tale in telling
it, and deliver a plain message bluntly: that which ordinary men
are fit for, I am qualified in, and the best of me is diligence.

LEAR
How old art thou?

KENT
Not so young, sir, as to love a woman for singing, nor so old to
dote on her for any thing: I have years on my back forty-eight.

LEAR
Follow me; thou shalt serve me: if I like thee no worse after
dinner, I will not part from thee yet. Dinner, ho, dinner! Where's
my knave? My fool? Go you, and call my fool hither.

Now, remember Shakespeare wrote for ear and eye: in this scene
the stage goes from empty to Kent alone in a royal hall; then with
bustle and horns Lear leads in a crowd of jostling courtiers, as Kent
catches Lear's eye, and the king asks him not "Who art thou?" but
"WHAT art thou?"

Kent's answer startles the king into asking once more, "What art
thou?"

Meantime, courtiers and nobles are *sotto voce* talking with each other
and in motion, drawing the eye away from the principals, a distraction
just convincing enough so that Kent's disguise passes. But in both
performances, watching several times, I found it hard to focus on Kent
and the King amid the hubbub. That interview is vital to the play; I was
surprised that an alert director did not subordinate the background
action or perhaps so space the actors that Kent and the King stood
forward, away from the crowding court.

In the two performances I watched, Olivier and Welles went

through their lines flawlessly, but at a speed that gave them no time to emphasize key words—it all flowed at one pitch.

Kent replies with enough, but not too much: he understands authority, including impaired authority; he speaks plainly, in good faith; he has experience of the world but is ready to learn more; he is ready to serve his liege lord. He twice answers Lear's repeated "What art thou?" Kent's speech implies good nature and a generous heart.

But in the play to follow, these qualities cannot stem the evils pursued by his monstrous opponents. Greed and madness have to work through their own hells. We are never to be other than human and at risk—of ourselves and each other.

A Shakespeare scholar may know more scenes reflecting apprenticeship, but my searching has found only one so direct. The word itself, hung out like a flag, is in Richard II, Act I, Scene III: Bolingbroke, son of the warrior John of Gaunt, is banished to exile by Richard and laments to his father:

Nay, rather, every tedious stride I make
Will but remember me what a deal of world
I wander from the jewels that I love.
Must I not serve a long apprenticehood
To foreign passages, and in the end,
Having my freedom, boast of nothing else
But that I was a journeyman to grief?

Kings of course don't do what Paul Luke did. While his sons and Earl Dodge were capable lieutenants, Paul spent most of his days in the yard, working shoulder to shoulder with the crew, going to his office only as he had to.

5

Earl, Day One

By the time work-light, work-piece, workman and tools were crammed in the space available, I was sure all hands present could hear me sweat. I worked out Rule Three all by myself. The joiner you want must be able to fix the unscrewable to the unglueable while motionless. Since nothing but motion—perpetual, by choice—has ever warmed a foreman's heart, I knew it would be an instructive day. The lockers above the settee I knelt on inclined me to prayer: they were fronted in stained-glass dolphins. While they were liquor lockers, I had no doubt that the old boy who first filled a hole in his wall with stained glass had a soul full of supplication to unload. After ten minutes on complaining knees, so did I. I first tried to fix the shape of the space in my head. Wrong. Next, I measured *everything in it*, carefully noting down each dimension. Wrong again.

Flanked by the jewel-glass cases, the roughed-in box over the port settee wore an innocent open front, a deceptive curve of hull at its back, a thick vertical pipe down one corner, and was otherwise naked as my back felt at the moment. Inside it was to go "some glahss," two levels of good crystal (at that moment, a month of the wage I suddenly didn't know how to earn), one socketed, one suspended. Behind these would go a mirror, to add depth. No wire ran through the locker, but the combined glass would add to the light so rare in the depths of many yacht cabins. Finished with a generous helping of Waterford, it would be the portside focus of the main cabin. The yacht's people would spend much of their off-watch time living with it in plain sight. Wobbly or wonderful, my novice piece would be visible as any work installed by Earl or Paul himself. Another bit of Paulian psychology,

Wandelaar saloon casework, settee/bunk and service hatches beneath, October 1978.

I think; something on the order of "put him on the grill and see if he burns."

The grill, incidentally, is no metaphor: the flowing, rounded grace of a yacht hull is framed in wood or metal, each piece of stock equipped with hard, often sharp, edges in its early stages. If you suppose you might enjoy boatbuilding, first spend some time kneeling while pushing, often and rhythmically, against some fixed object in front of you—while your uncushioned knees, perhaps your shins, "rest" on other edgy objects.

That you are building something worthwhile and beautiful and lasting will not somehow compensate for the agonies you may—unwarned—incur while doing this for extended periods, or the residual damage to your body. If you intend to build a boat, keep some padding—really sturdy padding—at hand. At the very least, your legs will live longer.

Earl understood the pain in my prayerful position. After all, he himself had spent years on his knees in boats. Two things kept me at it. Having said the unthinkable "I can do that," I would not last long if I didn't. Next (and easier to think about) the air inside the hull was solid empathy, with quiet amusement leaking through. Everyone there had gone through some form of this drill; I was only the latest prospect. In less than five minutes, the latest prospect understood painfully well that a yacht, in one of its many forms, is a careful assemblage of small, fascinating boxes, delighting by reason of their mutation in size and shape: I was hooked and baffled and trying, and they knew it.

Back to Earl—and Rule Two.

Scene One is still so present I tense up thinking about it. Scene One, this first morning, is set in church—the joiner shop. As lights go up, we see Earl, stage center amid knights and squires, firing short bursts of goodwill and tactics. (I will learn that while Earl is strategy itself, he delivers nothing but tactics to his troops and very brief tactics at that.) Earl stands, a boulder, rocking slightly alongside a glue-frame loaded with a month's pay in varnished cabinetwork, locker doors ready for installation.

Enter Paul Luke with new page in tow. Dressed in modest tabard and leggings (frayed shirt and torn jeans), the eager page wears also a slung shoulder kit in which are pocketed many sharp points and polished edges, whetted for the moment. Briefly narrow-eyed at the absence of a tool tray (page-standard passport in the earldom), Earl musters a tight grin as he advances the Right Hand of Peace in greeting.

"Says he's a joinuh," Paul finishes his introduction.

Earl's smile widens, "Well, we'll see—" Hand gripped, the page finds himself on the verge of crashing sideways, tool-points first, against very expensive lumber. Almost. His weight comes to balance (barely, and with prayer); the grip relaxes at once; in two shakes it has learned what it wants to know. Abrupt tactics follow, but Earl arrows these over his shoulder as the page races after him toward the big shed, straining to hear past what sounds like anger in a man he's only just met.

Rule Two, in the form of a question: Can he hang on and keep his feet? I'd seen it done, and long ago had been victim myself and forgot the lesson. It all began before the Phoenicians. Dry land is hazardous enough, but the sea and its vessels are more so. No good skipper wants a crewman who can't keep his feet in a world of no straight lines, a planet of infinite motion. The man will injure himself or die or kill a companion.

But what nagged me, as we crouched, heads jammed in under the saloon (a deep sea boat's living room) deckhead, was those doors. Varnished and finished, they would normally be—here of all places—on a solid bench topped with at least a cushion of corrugated cardboard. Never, ever, in that condition would they be stacked loose on a rickety, glue-ridged set of slats in harm's way. It seemed not a wonderful time to begin practice on a boat this man had been building for nearly a year and a half. I'll leave it there for now.

Day One dismissed any doubt of Earl's authority but somehow set him at full boil. And I have yet to meet anyone who reached Day Two without surviving the slings and arrows of Day One. Earl and I learned a lot.

The naval architect will lay out major furniture in his accommodation plan: galley, all cabins, lockers, heads (seagoing toilets), dressers, berths, lighting. Probably three thousand years of traceable practice, experience, logic, and technology go into these plans (example: beware the athwartship berth, for a berth set crossways to the long axis and path of the vessel can make those of tender stomach very ill indeed). The very best plans are great art, simplifying the joiner's work.

Any plans stayed in the office. "Pattuhn an' box that pipe," Earl said briefly, a little heat going out of his voice. "Balance it with a box at the far side. Ask Paul how the glahss goes."

ZOOM he was gone, leaving cavity and apprentice agape. The back of the box repeated hull curvature, and my eye showed an even curve. My hand, though, could feel a steadily changing curve fore and aft, and downward from the deckhead (in this case, the under-surface of the weather deck). The inland woodshop began to look attractive again, but the thought vanished with Earl. I found an unclaimed scrap of cardboard and began to study the art of custom yacht finishing.

Books on boatbuilding are many, marvelous, sometimes beautiful, occasionally inspiring and can even be helpful. Not a boatbuilding book in disguise, this a story of the working days of a few men and women who, in this small yard, built boats through a traditional Maine winter. Just remember, a traditional Maine winter can be long, exasperating, sad, beautiful and funny in the same day. If any of this is that, maybe I have learned to tell a tale. And maybe, if I can catch bits of them working or talking, it will tell how some of them came here to do this, and why they wanted to. If I am to do any of that, I had better begin by confirming what you long since have noticed: I began dead ignorant of what a professional boatbuilder does and how he or she does it, and in only a few ways did I become less ignorant. I learned enough to think that no one ever learns it all, but that Paul Luke got close, and Stanley closer.

I learned enough to think some of the great custom boats (Herreshoff and a few since, including Paul's) are high art. I learned enough to think the art will continue, despite the odds. Finally, I am still convinced, years later, that some of these days taught me ways of useful thinking, the best of all possible lessons.

Perhaps one or two of the owners for whom Paul and Earl and the rest had made a home afloat will tell how they feel about Paul and their boats. But you will have to buy your boatbuilding manual somewhere else. I'd suggest only that you look over the field before you buy, and that you might do better to buy all you can of the back issues of *Fine Woodworking* and *Woodenboat* magazines. Both are archive resources on first-rate woodwork.

One hint: If the book you come to admire includes the information that a half-inch industrial drill can lock up and hurl its operator right off a hull, then its writer may very well have done serious boatbuilding and be worth listening to. Apart from the books, five years in the Steinway piano factory or a few years with a custom cabinetmaker will help more than anything else. One more item, before I get on with it: Most of the good books mention, but none emphasize, conventions. Conventions are the practices found steadily useful, the forms of structure found always strong and graceful. They can differ a little between builders, and neither God nor Saint Howard Chapelle (historian famous among saltwater lovers) nor I can help an apprentice there. The First Convention is: Abandon Longshore Habit, and the Second is Observe and Ask (in precisely that order). I should add that the Ruling Convention in this work begins with: "You mean t' say there's none in the stockroom?" and ends with, "Weyell-l-l, (sigh), you bettuh make one."

The number of "ones" in a custom-built floating fantasy will exceed your imagining—and my own. Earl's impressive departure from the cabin stopped all asking, so I fell back on Observe.

The work in place showed cabin finish screwed and glued into a framework of cleating, with the cleating fixed to hull framing or other inboard structure. Earl's speed in stuffing me into this box rattled me. At first I couldn't see how to begin. I was sure only of one thing: Earl did not want a leisurely, inspective apprentice waiting for a laundry list. I took a deep breath, picked up Earl's hasty pencil marks, and began a careful set of measurements for my pattern, struggling around the fill pipe running down through my sweaty cell.

Wrong. Stanley (the older gent seen during my second hoof-in-mouth attack) began to have spasms of throat-clearing. Busy setting another glory of grab rail, Stanley still had time to notice that the new boy's brain was in neutral or worse. After Earl's third hull-shaking exit, he spoke: "Jawn, is it?"

"Yessir." A little severe, maybe, but since my foreman's launching I'd heard only a steady antiphon of numbers from the switchboard, and the atmosphere was getting Gregorian. If Earl's mood was the local weather, I could see storm clouds building. I looked worriedly at Stanley.

"It might," not quite looking back at me, Stanley cleared his throat again, a comforting old-man sound in the dedicated, technical quiet, "ahem, might go easiuh t' set th' cleatin' fust." He thumbed a nonexistent drop of glue off his screwdriver and cranked into another screw.

I mumbled thanks—as Earl thundered on board once more, this time at a dead run—dropped my pattern and had marks on my cleating stock by the time our chief joiner whizzed through into a forward compartment. Passing aft again, he slowed visibly and wore, trotting up the ladder, not quite the Hammer-of-Thor face I despaired of changing.

Without cleats to rib my box, I was measuring a void, one absent corner of which lay in an elusive arc back of the fill pipe—measurements I'd had in one minute and should have gone straight to my rough pattern with a knife, trimming the cardboard to mold my first cleat to the hull curvature. Once cut, the pattern fit neatly, but I'd wasted a half-hour in what I'd supposed was precision, working without understanding. By noon, my sweatbox wore the frame of a crystal locker, and I could hitch a couple of names to faces. Also by noon, despite the delays induced by his new hand's uncertainties amid his drive to finish the boat, Earl was talking.

That's what the others said he was doing. As the others made new-man ventures around mouthfuls of sandwich in the wire shop, I doubted I would last the noon hour. Every sound I had heard from Earl was a rivet-gun noise of frustration and anger, spliced here and there with solid bolts of direction, fired like rabbit punches. I knew I could never match Earl's speed if I stayed a lifetime. I also knew I was watching a boatbuilding genius, a man who could teach me more in ten days than I could learn elsewhere in ten weeks. I knew both my knees were balloons and broken. I knew I didn't know anything. Having remembered that, I shut up, looking and listening with care.

By mid afternoon, absorbed in that never-the-same arc at the back of the case, I forgot my knees entirely. Reminded by the whistle at four, I staggered out to the car before anyone could hand me a pink slip, drove 130 miles round trip to fetch my wife and my tool chest, and finally went to my bed like a felled ox. One day of what I hoped was boatbuilding and I had a grip on only one thing: these people cared about their work *and* about the workman who came to it. And the eldest thought I might turn out all right, given time and prompting. It sounded that way.

I had seen this devotion—and my sense here includes "devout"—before: briefly in a laboratory and again in a peacetime Marine rifle platoon but never in any production system or situation and rarely in any church, apart from the solitary in consultation with his Maker.

Somehow I had stumbled into a builders' ark full of peers instead of pairs, and the only catch was Earl, who didn't think I had the makings of a good round curse, let alone one of his joiners. I had known by nightfall that Earl had been Paul's best right arm for thirty years, that he was to be asked ANY question, small or large, about the hull, before we approached Paul. How could a man given this authority be inflamed by shaking hands with a new employee? He went livid the instant he saw the little *ryoba*. (*Ryoba nokogiri*, a small handsaw, cutting on the pull stroke, one edge for crosscutting, the other, with larger and differently shaped teeth, for ripping with the long grain of a work-piece.) "Where'd y' get the Jap saw?"

"Mail order. Out of Seattle."

"SNORT!"

Long after, long lanky Bill told me it was the only day he could remember wiring a boat in a minefield. I couldn't hear the mutter after the snort, but Earl's stomp could be heard from the time he left the hull until the table saw tuned up in the joiner shop, three sheds off. A disembodied voice rose from under the owner's cabin steps, where young Steve hung head-down in a tangle of rainbow wire, "Just have to ignore it, John; he's this way every time we get a new man."

Maybe. While I worked for Paul, Earl had to tend a further handful of incoming new hands. He directed them all, day in, day out, without raising an eyebrow or his voice.

He had to let one of them go, when he found the man could read a clock at four p.m. but not at seven a.m. He managed it like an uncle. Something about me bit Earl, and it was not my lack of experience. Earl knew all that Paul knew, well before we shook hands. The only bits of relief I remember from that whole day were the empathy I sensed around me in the hull and the very strongest language that Earl used, ever, in my hearing, then or later—"Jesus, Jesus, Jesus," he whispered, standing alone in the joiner shop, as I came unheard along the drunken walkway from the next shed. It wasn't a curse. It was a prayer.

That night I fell asleep on an idea for the locker.

6

The Doctor's Maine Story

Two men, men so old they were walnut from frayed cap brim to buttoned shirt collar, lived across the road from each other most of their lives. Aside from a fall hunt together and some jaw-oiling applejack, they waved their good mornings and rarely spoke in the course of a set of seasons. Their children had left home; they had sold their sheep. The 1938 storm knocked hell out of their woodlots and timber, so both men had their pines cut and sawn. They ran dairy cows so long all the cows kept their mothers' names. Their wives died. They sold the horses and finally most of the cattle, each keeping only a milk cow. The fall hunt became troublesome, what with bad knees and sports from away, who for some years were apt to drop the hammer on anything that moved, farmers and stock not omitted. With the wives gone, neither had the heart to keep a dog anymore, and then the apples failed, two years running.

At morning chores, no matter the dark or light time of year, Ansel waved to Hiram from his barn door. At evening chores, Hiram waved to Ansel from the path grooved between barn and house. One morning, Ansel didn't wave. Wasn't anywhere in sight. Hiram thought about this at length but decided he and his friend were getting to the age where an urgent bladder might make either of them a little absentminded. He had read that this happened, when you got on a little. So at evening chores, Hiram waited outside his door near fifteen minutes, hoping Ansel would show against the dark barn across the road. No lamp or light showed at his friend's house.

Hiram began to worry. He located his lantern and finally the can of kerosene he'd mislaid last spring. He snapped the match across his thumbnail, lit the lantern, and crossed the road.

Junior Witham from the VFW managed to drag them both out before the barn roof went, but it took most of the night to sort it out. Hiram didn't wake until near morning. The doc didn't get much out of Junior, except he found Ansel pinned to the floor by his haymow fork, Hiram out cold on the floor beside him, and the barn lighting up the township. Junior had his mind on the Senior Citizens' Annual Eight-Ball Tournament at the VFW that night and wanted to discuss his bank-shot, the one that took out the mirruh and ol' Waltuh's hat aftuh it sunk the one-ball. Waltuh got awful ugly 'bout it. Wantid his entry fee back and a fresh drink.

With the hole in Ansel's arm laced up and a pint of blood for luck, the doctor roused him. The old eyes flickered open on thick cataracts. "Ansel, how'd you do that?"

"Stumbled."

"Well, didn't you yell for Hiram?"

"Heyell yes, 'il I passed aout."

"Hnh—man in your condition, we can do something about your eyes. How old're you, Ansel?"

"Ettynine come Octobuh, why?"

"Jesus Christ," murmured the doctor. "You hurt anywhere else?"

"Just m' pride. Kin I git outa heah?"

"NO, dammit, you stay put. Tonight anyhow."

Toward morning the doctor came back to find Hiram studying the ceiling, running one hand and then the other over his strapped ribs and bandaged scalp. "Hiram, what happened?"

"Dam' caow tore loothe of 'er haltuh. Got me right in th' arthe on 'er way aout. Druv me up agin the fawk."

"You didn't hear her comin'?"

"Heyell no. Ain't heard nothin' in thutty yeahth."

"How did you—you read lips?"

"Ayeh."

"Jesus Christ!"

"Thouldn't cary on tho, doctuh."

"Howinhell old're you, Hiram?"

"Dunno," Hiram stroked his scalp again, " 'bout ninety-one, I think."

"Jesus Christ!"

"Naow, doctuh."

The doctor turned to Ansel, "Ansel, I'm sorry, the boys say your barn's gone. They saved the house."

"Ayeh."

Hiram grunted his way onto one elbow and waved at Ansel, "What'd he thay?"

"He says THE BARN BURNT!"

"Thorry, Anthel. Muthta got abthent-minded," the older man gummed.

"It's all right!" Ansel roared happily, I 'membered the damn insurance f'once!"

"Jesus Christ!" marveled the doctor.

"BESIDES!" Ansel persisted, at a volume that brought the duty nurse running, "Th' APPLES DID GOOD THIS YEAH! AND WE'RE ALIVE, AIN'T WE?"

"Ayeh," said Hiram, grinning pinkly.

"Jesus Christ Almighty!" said the doctor, striding out to schedule Ansel for eye surgery. The doctor called this his "Jesus Christ Maine Story" and says it really firmed up his faith in a theory he heard shortly after bringing his degree north: "If you can't stand the nails, you better get off the cross."

7

Early August

So. It is early August. I'm working with (most of the time) a handful of men and one young woman, Becky, who finish-sands and varnishes most of what we do. A couple of days make it plain that most of what we say in the yard, the boat, and the shop—sometimes with the exception of lunch hour—will deal with work. In Paul's yard a surprising amount of time could pass, with five or six working in the boat, with no conversation at all. Compensation for this most often showed up at lunchtime, when the day's crew gathered themselves into the warmth of the winter wire shop, which abutted the joiner shop.

Work with one's hands in no way stills the mind. If you're observant by nature or habit, your observations will produce thought, sometimes even ideas. If you've come this far with me, you are willing to hear some of what was expanding—or disturbing—my mind at the time. And with this in hand, the rest of my story may make better sense—not simpler, I think, but better.

* * *

A custom yacht can be a soul-satisfying thing. In modest size it can be built by a few hands, but in magnum size it will be the product of many. The variety of suppliers one needs for the creation of her varied equipment will multiply almost beyond counting by the time she settles in the water. If she is a big boat, she will need an ant farm of builders to bring her to launching in what all concerned hope will be a reasonable time.

Like artist and artisan the world around, I came to this place wanting to do work that made me happy and that contributed to the happiness of others. I hoped to earn a living wage, and for most of that year was in fact just able to do so. My great compensation came in the sheer whelming knowledge of fine joinery surrounding me every day.

In writing my story I'll keep to sequence for the most part. A few asides tell less about building and more about the builders. "Why" to me remains one of the most important words in our language, so there are a few pages of why, and they may or may not resemble what is in front of you right now.

In a book titled *Of Whales and Men*, the story of a modern pelagic whaling expedition to the Antarctic, R. B. Robertson, MD, identifies a condition he finds widespread in the crew. Like Robertson's people, mine are men and women who appear in some degree to have a "suffering mind," literally sick of the drone and dross of civilization, driven to do what they can with what they have, and in every practical sense dedicated to doing or being or building something different, perhaps something that will comfort if not satisfy their minds.

A cruising yacht, beyond its aspect as a private sailing vehicle aboard which one can live in comfort while making long passages, is often a beautiful object, which for many owners is sufficient to ease what ails them. Over several seasons, I crewed for the owner/skipper of a lovely folkboat, a sloop on which he and his wife sailed weekends and raced on other weekends. I was most often crew/live ballast for a race, which gave me lots of time to admire other boats. We sailed out of Sausalito—this in the '60s—a sheltered port on San Francisco Bay, whose shore even then was lined five and ten deep with sail and motor yachts, at least half of which seemed never to leave their berths, no matter fair or foul weather or ambient sailing conditions. Objects. Ornaments—

Given the right owner, a cruising yacht can be a far greater thing, a body of knowledge, a teacher of self-knowledge, a path to understanding, a vessel able to extend one's world, real or virtual or both.

In my eighth decade my philosophy is pleased if it can come to grips with small things. Most vessels for recreation are a size suited to building by a few pairs of hands, working or playing in concert. Paul's yard seldom had more than fifteen people working at one time.

I don't suppose Presbyterian deacons built the clipper ships *Flying Cloud* or *Lightning* or that many of the hands that put them together stayed sober on their way home from work. But a lot of caring and even thoughtful hands were involved, and the hand and its work—forever, amen!—are the outward expression of the mind. In those vessels were minds absorbed in the shape of every framing timber, every length of saloon molding, every tall spar. I still think life might be more rewarding if one callused palm that helped build the royal ship of Khufu or the Gokstad Viking ship, or George Steers' *America* had been impractical enough to write down what it felt like to hang a sheer plank. Because I still don't know. Until very recently, builders built and writers wrote, and they seldom crossed paths.

More often now our makers and doers can and will write. And I think when they do, our view improves.

It strikes me that mainly due to ancient faith and beliefs do we have any glimpses into the eldest of these breathtaking monuments out of the mist. But here they are, sculpted, solid, touchable, the powerful speech of ancient minds. Will we be so lucky again? Will the apprentice show up?

Robert Blackburn Robertson, MD, was senior medical officer and de facto company psychiatrist for the 1950–51 Antarctic whaling expedition of a British corporation (not named in his book), which employed 650 Scottish and Norwegian whalemen on that voyage alone. Robertson begins his book with a quote from a Captain C. B. Hawes, whose belief it was that "the old whaling vessels had more than their arithmetical proportion of madmen."

Robertson's first chapter opens with, "Some twelve thousand men go down to the Southern Ocean each year to hunt the whale." You can see why he felt that a psychological affliction might be involved here, and he was interested enough to apply for his post as doctor.

I have never met anyone willing to sail twenty thousand miles to do their daily work among krill and icebergs so large they could nudge Scotland toward Norway by three inches at a bump. Especially when that daily work involved the killing and dismembering of the biggest animal ever to live on earth.

His book is cheerful, but without mistake the result of a desire to observe the behaviors of the whalemen he was sure were endowed with some form of psychopathy. I hadn't his excuse for my winter in Paul's yard. I desperately needed work of some kind that would keep me sane and absorbed, possibly teach me something, and please me when done. The men and women who came with the job were a gift, one of the best I've had in my life and unlike anyone I knew before. They taught me in what I've come to think may be the best way possible. They let me learn things I could not have learned any other way with the sureness they left in my hands. As a journeyman cabinetmaker unschooled in psychology, I suppose the nature of the place we worked in did hold an attraction for some unease that can reach the strength of compulsion. I'm a book addict, so my hero list holds many writers. All of course are flawed, for one reason or another, all fabled, some for their flaws, all possessed of a vision of the possible, while aware, painfully in most cases, of the world they could see every day—a world they wrote about, most from compulsion.

Among the anonymous heroes of equal fame, I place together the last editor to drip candle wax on what became the King James Bible and the Norseman who saw water move so clearly that he was able to hew out the shape that became the Viking longship. And perhaps Miguel de Cervantes, more wonderful than any in representing the man or woman aware that beyond here is a place dangerous but special, better for learning, for preserving a little more grace in a world bent on strife. I'm looking for a definition here, because Robertson spoke mostly of the man or woman "with suffering mind," looking for escape or release from at least a few of the evils our civilization carries and spawns. His minds were the crews of the whaling factory ship and the relatively tiny catcher boats, at risk all day every day in some of the deadliest saltwater on the planet.

Not much question but a suffering mind or two came to the Luke yard over its years of building, my own among them. But my impression is that we were looking for a launching toward, as much as for a release from. Release from a sameness increasingly deadly to mind and spirit, release to a larger knowledge, a wider perspective, a better understanding, somehow set in these aluminum whales filled with curious space, with wire and wood, with nerve and skill and spirit, we hoped, work, workmanship, and maybe even wisdom.

What a lot to ask of a boat. What a lot to put into a boat. If this sounds overcooked—hunting wisdom in a shipyard—then I have to keep going. In just such a place was made Homer's entire fleet, Cleopatra's floating palace, the Viking longship, Sir Francis Drake *Golden Hind*, James Cook's *Endeavour*, the frigate USS *Constitution*, the tea clipper *Cutty Sark*, Donald McKay's *Lightning*, the schooner yacht *America*—vessels to gather, to carry, to fight, for what?

Some of my heat probably comes from the troubling places I passed through on my way to the Luke yard, some dulling, exasperating, some just stupefying; some of my heat surely comes from the time I arrived at the yard, unsure, a little scared by all these professionals, who, you can be sure, were there chiefly to build and to learn to build, like myself. All I can tell you about the rest of what they came for is this: Building good things lifts the spirit, even if you happen to find glue drooling on you from a job overhead. Destroying things will, soon or late, freeze and diminish the spirit and, continued long enough, destroy the person. And while I could find no way to say this clearly before now, my first impression of Paul's yard was, "These people are crazy to build good stuff!" And I wanted to learn how.

*   *   *

The everyday news in 1977–78 had much the dull ring of turmoil we see in newspapers and on TV in 1998–99 and on into the present day. James Earl Carter was our president; his U.N. ambassador, Andrew Young, was publicly calling Richard Nixon and Gerald Ford racist; Judge Sirica signed an order requiring former Attorney General John Mitchell and Nixon aide H. R. Haldeman to begin serving their prison sentences; columnist Jack Anderson observed that "Bureaucrats Buck Carter"; and that good man Leon Jaworski surfaced in a UPI story, claiming that South Korea sought to buy influence in Congress.

Researching lately to see what I was NOT conscious of—in fact, a great deal—in the days of trying to become a useful tool in a shipyard, I have the frustrating feeling that we live today in recycled history, sucked out of a twenty-year-old newspaper, or *60 Minutes*, pumped forward just years enough to splash or leak into tomorrow's news headline, tonight's six o'clock infotainment. The next thought, however, takes pride of place: Not once in my shipyard time, no matter there were several kinds of repetitious labor, did I ever think to myself, I've been here and done this and I'm BORED. Not one single time, including the days we spent smelting lead out of old nets and desiccated fish guts. After all, a good boat needs a good keel, yes? Noses running, eyes streaming, heads reeling in the thick stink, we hauled old lead to the burner.

*   *   *

Wandelaar port-side saloon crystal case, surface woodwork by Stanley Mitchell, interior center case by author, August 1978.

After a few days, the saloon of the silver whale had an open-front crystal locker, ready to sail on its starboard ear in any but all-hands weather without harm to glass or crew. Paul and Earl took infinite pains to see this done, also to make sure any glass could be removed without touching its neighbor. Their infinite pains most of the time had just involved a sharp glance in passing, but if my cardboard pattern failed to pass inspection or if I seemed uncertain or dawdling, Stanley's throat would clear or Earl's eyebrows furrow to a militant alarm in time to warn me off whatever stupidity I was committing. The smooth butternut coaming around the locker aperture remained uninjured, but I'm not sure why.

Every instant I wasn't taking pains I was watching Stanley. Stanley always had a smile and a "good morning" but little conversation beyond our first one. In spite of this, his moldings and drawer fronts and grab rails ten feet away went sliding through my fingers into the crystal locker. Telekinesis works; don't disturb a useful illusion or whatever it is that helps it work. And it eased the pains I took so much that out of all the pieces I put in that boat, at this writing I can't remember the feel of one single stick I put into that locker.

Back in church, I finish-sanded the hanger plate as Earl skidded to a stop at his bench. Turning toward him, I dangled a goblet in the plate and let the result flop ninety degrees. His hand snaked out, but the glass stayed put. He squinted at me, a squint that might have been a grin, and muttered, "Put it in." I was clear of the joiner shop when I heard, "Start hangin' th' lockah doors."

* * *

"You got a butt gauge?" I had an armload of doors, and the squint was not hiding a grin.

"No." I not only didn't have a butt gauge, I'd never seen or heard of the item. Earl's eyebrows confirmed his tone of voice. The village idiot was still present. I shouldn't have done the glass trick—it set him thinking. Earl thinking boat could outthink any man in the shop, which of course he was paid to do. I had met foremen who were seriously overpaid, but never once did Earl even seem to qualify for anything but the reverse of that opinion. Clutching the doors, I waited for the blast. The squint changed, not to a glower but a look of disappointment.

"Nevuh heard of a joinuh didn't hev a butt gauge," he grumped. "Well, hang th' doors, anyway." He leaped for the stair to the timber stack.

I staggered toward the big shed and the boat, invoking deities and trying to invoke memory. I suppose I hung doors the rest of that Friday. They were safely in place Monday, I noticed, and wedged shut to keep them from harm until catches could be installed. Another reproof, I guessed, though nothing was said.

My memory of Friday was the cursed "I can do that" echoing, and what on earth was a butt gauge? By day's end I hadn't figured out a way to ask without reinforcing local opinion of the new boy's sketchy equipment. Earl's eye had flared again when I offered my steel pocket rule. It was then I learned that all hands but myself were so talented they could measure a sixty-five-foot yacht with an old-fashioned two-foot folding rule, "An' howcum you don't hev THAT, eithuh?"

By quitting time Friday, I had a gargantuan headful of "butt gauge" and other evils, among them a real sense of hopelessness. I'd stopped thinking. I also had a paycheck and no pink slip. Dazzled, I levitated my week's collection of bumps and bruises across the parking lot without leaving a footprint and drove home confused and full of butt gauges.

Monday morning I had a butt gauge, four opinions on its use, and at last the sense to ask Earl how HE wanted it used. He was so startled he was almost voluble—but recovered in a minute or so. I spent days hanging doors, setting locker catches, inspecting endless boxes I hadn't seen before. In the sixty-five feet of the silver whale, no bunk was more than eight steps from a flush, and while pump handles were mounted, waste was tanked or sent overboard with the push of a button.

While all the beautiful butternut was swinging into place, Paul developed a rising enthusiasm for getting the boat done. My days that week were fairly peaceful but for the moments when my employer's eye lit on his newest and slowest joiner. The least glance seemed to double his enthusiasm, no matter where he found me, and his enthusiasm began to permeate the whole shop. At one point I thought I saw a mouse hauling lumber, but when I got my dusty glasses off I found Becky from the paint shop trying to clear herself a path through the rising wreckage in the joiner shop.

By midweek even Earl was looking black, muttering under his breath for reasons other than myself. I was trying to turn into Becky's mouse, and several hands almost managed invisibility: where Paul was, they were not. Building boats takes time. Building custom yachts takes more time. Building a big custom yacht to her architect's implacable specifications, federal environmental demands, Coast Guard charter regulations, and fitting her out to Lloyds' 100-A1 and her owner's more skyward ideals as to what constitutes a proper yacht takes an appalling amount of time. Every contractor's time is money, so while Paul was invoking every tongue but money, it began to sound as if he was having a severe case of contract. His cries of encouragement made Billy think he might be looking at overtime penalties, but this was ventured the way Billy preferred to say a thing: a little tentative and a long way from Paul.

Not that anything else could have been heard with our leader present. Murphy's Law this time had taken the form of unproductive manufacturers, vacationing wholesalers, and erratic common carriers. At some point we heard that a whimsical dispatcher had aimed a trailer full of gear for Paul at Portland, Oregon. We improved the few silences in the next week by routing the same load through Awful, OK, Bungle, TN, Crash, CO, Dismal, MO, Help, MI, Near, MS, and Tellme, WY, but humor was no help. Paul couldn't wait for the trucks, and the few invoices and manifests to reach him only lengthened his face and strengthened his enthusiasm. All of us had sandpaper ears by the time he decided to make a foraging tour that we hoped would relieve him, them, it, or us. It turned out to be mostly us, but while he was gone I came to appreciate more than ever why a custom yacht, given any care at all by her owners, lasts longer than most floatables. By the time she is launched, Murphy has had a nervous breakdown and needs years to recover.

A week in any manufacturing plant will produce this list or its near cousin: with everything set up, you step on your work-lamp plug and must go to the far end of the shop to find a screw small enough to fix it. With that done, you find you also pulled the wire from one side of the socket, so must fix this, too.

There is not one single 3/4 inch number 8 stainless woodscrew in the yard. A furious half-hour search finds the four you must have. Never mind where they came from, beyond a shelf in the stockroom.

You come second in line to the one accurate table saw: next behind you is your foreman, and why are you standing there sucking your thumb?

The next waffle you want is (a) at the bottom of a heap of fourteen woefuls you do not want, (b) at the farthest extremity of the shop from where you find you need it, (c) mislaid while you "bear a hand here" en route, or (d) takes three of you an hour hunting before the boss himself remembers he used the last waffle yesterday.

As a last resort, you go to your leader's right-hand man (often a woman) for help. It was rare that Paul's Barbara could not cure a loss or absence of needed materials or at the very least limit the hunt: "He knows better'n that, we used 'em up a week ago!" If she didn't have a perfect mental file on every part in the yard, she at least had perfected the art of distracting Paul until she knew where the absent piece lay or until she could put it in his hand.

Another man has the little plank-end you set aside for a certain glamorous piece of work. In fact, he has a crowbar in it and is moving a ton of overhead mill across it on spiked rollers. Earl is allowed comment here, but an apprentice? Go humble back to the timber stacks.

Back on board, the screwdriver you laid safe on the galley counter has vanished. You use another that doesn't quite fit. It slips. You remove eight screws, trot back to church, plane out the divot, trudge back and install with greater care. The next man into the engine room below kneels in the bilges. Your absent screwdriver leaves a half-inch hole in his jeans. He objects to the new-boy habit of square corners on the driver-bit. You object to the old-hand habit of dropping into black holes without a work lamp.

You slang each other a minute or so, a pair of seagulls wrangling fish-bait. On turning, you find the name-calling face rising from the hatch is wearing a fox-grin, his lamp lit, and no torn jeans at all. He allows his own screwdrivers are pretty disgraceful, and thanks for the loan.

A howl reinforced with crashing lumber under the hull orders you to fetch a 2 by 6. Nowhere in timber storage is there a 2 by 6 by 12 feet or of any length. Not in this yard, not in Boothbay, and possibly not in Lincoln County, Maine. You cut one from wider stock, which has to be power-planed—after you find the blown fuse. On your return, you find that Earl has one, has strong views on the length of your afternoon nap, and why didn't you bring three? He's sure he said three. Oh, well. Your own version of the boss who helped Noah plank the Ark mutters that the last piece you did looks pretty fair. An hour later Earl wants to know what you're grinning about. Finally a question you can ignore, because he knows, too. And someone else brings his next frown.

The more you learn, the more you must learn. Multiply by ten for this yard, divide by no time to think about it, and remember how you felt about punching machinery and pushing paper forever. If you are new at factories—and in spite of onrushing middle age, I was very new—the Left-Handed Monkey Wrench will finally put in an appearance. This has been an Essential Tool of Industry since Merlin's ancestors contracted Stonehenge, so I was fairly sure I'd recognize it when it showed up. On the day it appeared, I had made six complete searches of Paul's multilevel widget-warren and had found only one item I was sent for. "Get me the half-inch-right-angle drill out of the machine shop."

I stared at Earl, stunned. Anybody but him. I was full of doubt, exasperation, suspicion, and exhaustion: in three and a half hours I'd spent fifteen minutes on one shelf and the rest of the time raising dust and distance from my assignment. If this was the local version of the General Motors orientation course, I was getting damned tired of it. More alarming, his face crinkled into something I didn't recognize at first.

He was smiling. "Go on," he said calmly, "a half-inch-right-angle. I'm serious." Doubtful, I nodded and trudged off the hull. With all three fans going (for once), the heat inside the hull was a misery and the rest of the shop not much better. In the machine shop, Tom grinned at me, swore there really was a right-angle drill—that he'd used it that day—and he thought Stover had it now. Tom was a little less new than myself, moved here from New Jersey, and so reassuring I began to believe him. Stover, a stair and two sheds off, did not have the drill: he had put it back, he said. Aware by now that only Earl ever left a tool where he got it, I staggered the length of the crazy walkway once more and excavated the bench Stover said he left it on. No drill. Back to church: it wasn't even in the heaped corner where we left electric tools for repair. It was, finally, just outside the joiner shop, under *Sea Swallow*, with a young crank on the end of it glaring defensively. It had just twisted his wrist, and while he would be glad to be shut of it, he had to finish this series of holes. I helped him brace the beast. As the whistle blew, Earl arrived, glaring at both of us. In perfect unison, the three of us shrugged, shook our heads, and left work for the day. Another week like this, and they'd take me out in a basket, if one could be found.

I began to wonder if the books held any wisdom about preserving elbows, patience, knees, or courage. In this department, "Observe and Ask" was getting nowhere. So far, any part of the boat I approached would lunge at me when I wasn't looking, and after Day One I stopped counting scars from the knees down. This in a boat so near done we were fitting her cabins with furniture; how would I survive the endless framing of a new hull?

Boatbuilding by Howard Chapelle is crusty, determined, pedantic, and orderly for 202 pages, but if you check pages 22 and 23 you will find him able to slip off his celluloid collar and sleeve garters, while he says exactly how it gets done.

> The most important requirements in a builder are accuracy and patience. The beginner should have no feeling of haste. He must plan each operation well in advance and try to see not only that . . . job but the one following it; by this means he will avoid having to undo some work already completed in order to get at a fastening, or to fit some member later on.
>
> In every amateur boatbuilder's shop there should be a "moaning chair"; this should be a comfortable seat from which the boat can be easily seen and in which the builder can sit, smoke, chew, drink or swear as the moment demands.

Here he should rest often and think about his next job. The
plans should be at hand and here he can lay out his work. By
so doing he will often be able to see mistakes before they are
serious and avoid the curse of all amateur boatbuilders: starting
a job before figuring out what has to be done to get it right.

Without knowing about moaning chairs, I'd seen several in my
first week with the crew. In this case, of course, they were highly
professional moaning chairs, and in short order I had my own. It also
dawned on me that while I'd been fitting out, sailing and generally
messing about in boats for years, I had only the barest idea of a basic
definition of "boat." And if I thought myself crazy to be building an
object I couldn't define, what was Paul thinking?

8

The Name of the Thing

Recovered from his exercise over the missing trailer full of gear "for Portland," Paul was thinking boat, spars, and launching, but mostly boat. Apart from his daily business of phones and paper and visitors, Paul worked with his crew, probably the simplest way of knowing at a glance what was done, where he should push next, and how Earl, Stanley and the rest of us were handling it.

But while I have loved boats all my life, I could not then have given a crisp definition of either "boat" or "yacht," although I knew the latter derived from a Dutch word that has to do with hunting. At home visiting my mother, I dug out the stored cases of books.

"A vessel for transport by water," said my Random House dictionary, "constructed to provide buoyancy by excluding water and shaped to give stability and permit propulsion."

Well, yes . . . and that covers the *Titanic*, too, meant to provide state-of-the-art buoyancy—a magnificent vessel, drowned by hubris, at no fault of her builders. Maybe that definition is a bit too crisp; "with intent" might well have been added just after "constructed."

Titanic was certainly built with intent. Was Paul's endless uproar the result of knowing that one day his masterpiece would find a First Officer Murdock to test it? This didn't fit. In my few days with him, I'd confirmed that one of Paul's hulls brought all her people back after her keel turned sail for a deadly few moments in mid ocean. Only very strong vessels for transport by water come home from a pitchpoling, whatever the quality of their crew. This man knew what he did, and he did it with diligence and better than most.

"Yacht," Random House goes on, "a vessel used for private

cruising, racing, and other non-commercial purposes." Good, but like the first, not quite so. With chartering, less legal (but greener) ventures, and the extractive talent of most taxation systems, every yachtsman not rolling in cash is, for at least part of the ship's life, devising ways to make her pay. Modern definitions of "yacht" are legion, but this keeled château damaging Paul's vocal cords had roots far deeper than Paul, and covered more vessels than Billy's perfect painting skills.

The celluloid collars and pince-nez scholars in my *Webster's Second International* understood my question. "Noun," it says, and I paraphrase: from the Dutch, *jacht*, from the earlier Dutch, *jaght*, short for *jaghtschip*, pursuit ship (originally against pirates), from *jaght*, pursuit, chase, hunting . . . "Nautical origin, a ship of light draft built to sail with speed; now, any one of various types of relatively small vessels, characteristically with sharp prow and graceful lines, and ordinarily privately owned and used for pleasure."

Pursuit. Chase. Hunting. Leave it to the practical Dutch to nail down with one symbol what every yacht-person since Khufu must have somewhere in mind. The pursuit of something essential, something not to be had elsewhere?

Inside one's self, between wind and water, classically, and I suspect a logician could sustain the argument, a yacht is no luxury at all but an absolute necessity. A private external miniature world, then, built with intent to pursue one or more internal aims. If my employer was putting all that under canvas, I could understand why Earl got nervous every time he looked at me.

Old Noah's copperplate pen doesn't fumble the adjective, either: "custom" work is "made or done to order." It is work made face-to-face and hand-to-hand, with all parties determined to see Murphy and his Law in Hell. Custom is the personal art, Paul's thumbprint, etched and inked through Earl, struck by all hands in the yard, looming tall and bold in the spider-scaffold of the shed.

Paul's work and yard were not related to the style of custom yacht where a three-bedroom ranch is shoehorned into some curiously curved form, seen by some as the Noah's Urp School of Naval Architecture. But these also are sold and sailed: somebody loves them.

The labor of the men and women working for the remaining Paul Lukes is not prepackaged. They do not fill a standard form; they work to fill a model of experience and experiment.

With each contract signed, the yard's work begins with two

meticulous, straight lines. The first is drawn on the snowfield of the fresh-paint floor of the mold loft, a flat world drawn to full scale by Earl working with one helper. Out in the shed, a big steel beam is set horizontal at a predetermined height, and the same line scored on it or hung taut above it. Every boat dimension is drawn from the loft line, measured from its twin in the shed over and over again, and every man jack of us was told by Earl that he expected every measurement he made to register within 1/32nd of an inch.

From this second line grows a set of solids in the air of Paul's yard, surfaces in space, the bone, bulk and belly of an aluminum whale, a workaday sum of the last mathematics of ancient romance and a sea-kindly cup. Her builders are the only people who will truly see and know all of her, spine, heart, nerve, sinew, and skin; they take the owner's idea, the architect's art, and make of these bone and brawn and finally life itself, the last and best magic. "It" becomes "she," and of course we fall in love with her.

"You bitch!" snaps Bill, tugging a fistful of her nerve-ends, finding blood on his knuckle. Bill is a lank six feet, patient, mostly quiet, not given to these endearments unless really tired or exasperated or both. He goes to find the first-aid box, while Steve screws down a connector bar to which more wire will go.

Becky paints and varnishes with Billy. She is the only woman steadily with the crew. She has a vocabulary rich as any in the yard, but somehow not as much provocation to use it. Her presence on or in the boat always abbreviates cursing but doesn't stop it. She is an increasingly apt painter, schooled by Billy and Paul both, but Earl still shakes his head, "Odearodearodear," and does not let her near a woodworking tool. Becky adores Stanley and watches every working motion he makes as she passes his bench in the joiner shop.

Unobserved, I hear a whispered "You miserable sh—" as Steve addresses a large pump of uncertain gender with vigor and the heaviest wrench he can find. Which had just slipped, painfully.

"Big dam' whoah," Billy sighs, staggering past with another bucket of God-knows-what he's using to fair one of her larger plates. Whore she is, measure and altar of their years, however mixed their feelings and my metaphors. They will drive through blizzards to lay with their whore. Without thinking much about it, often without thinking at all beyond the next job to be done, they return to worship. On many days there is a point of exhaustion beyond which they cannot think; hatred sets in, hatred for the job, the boat, each other, themselves. Ourselves. And we are back the next morning working, to worship harder—if possible—than before, praying louder.

"Ah-h, she's a paycheck. Handy to home."

At one point a tanned, slim, intense man drove from Texas to Paul's to learn the proper building of boats. He had got tired of being a surgeon, which may be why he later kept my knee from being crushed by a sliding timber. Billy's "handy to home" doesn't answer Doug's quest: We come hunting from far places, take less than we could earn at equally demanding work done in relative comfort. In some way, she is offering and chalice, child and mandala, and we scold her with curse and sexual insult, because we begin to love the creature we invest with so much of our self and our care. On her way to water, she becomes our profession of faith.

Some days the exhaustion around her by late afternoon is complete, the faces gray as those at a fatal fire, as those on troops who somehow came back alive. But she daily makes us small gods, building an infant world, nursing her toward her element. The moment I suggested this, I was a nitwit again, Billy eying me carefully, checking for new thickets of wild hair. "Jist a bo't," he muttered, retreating quickly to the paint shop and safety.

And an eagle, after all, is just a bird. Behavior suggests something else. The sheds are mortuary, when she goes: cleaning and gloom, make-work and gloom, sorting and gloom, restocking and gloom. No layoffs. To the brink and a cable-length after, Paul and his peers keep their men, their madmen, and find ways to keep them busy until a shaft of sun strikes fresh, white paint and a new, harsh, unbending line down the long loft floor. Whether they like or dislike each other, Paul and his peers and their people hang on for that line, that simple line of endless complexity. It is quality and instinct, and they wither only if you ask them for less.

A few days after the crystal locker was done, Earl wanted a finish top on the navigation desk. One edge of this had, as always, to fit snug against one end of a saloon settee/bunk. Tony, youngest of the crew, examined my efforts toward a matching edge and shook his head three times before he thought it right to drill holes for the screws to snug it down. I didn't argue.

Then I had to go back to the joiner shop and plane my edge one more time. The vertical plate I was matching, meant to be flat, could only be fitted tight if the edge of my horizontal plate made an almost invisible convex figure. If my edge was straight, the doghouse windows shed a light so wonderful that a dark gap suggesting an archer's bow lay at the fugitive joint.

The joiner who fitted up the bunk had forgotten only one thing—to check his surface with a straight edge before he glued it and clamped up. Tony was a young man with manners, so his urging ran more to, "Gee, I'd try shaving it over here," as opposed to the military-industrial explicitudes more familiar to me. And the uncommon good cheer on his normally sober round face after I got it right made it a smaller chore than it could have been.

It didn't occur to me until later to wonder who might have installed the bunk.

Tony in those weeks spent a lot of time dealing with Formica in big sheets, fitting it to impossible intersecting angles in the several heads on this jewel of nautical plumbing. But he had time to watch what the new boy was up to and make sure he was up to snuff. Nothing we did had any relation to how the owner might feel about the result. It had everything to do with workmanlike and with what we would want to see every day if we should ever own such a boat. Art was never mentioned in my hearing in that yard. Workmanship was the driving force, and while it was sometimes joked about, it was there all day every day.

I've said that Tony was youngest of the joiner crew. Did this show up in his finished work? Never. As with the rest of us, process and product were examined all day every day, and he and I alike sweated two things: a perfect fit, followed by a look and a nod the next time Earl or Stanley came past. Nothing else. Well, ALMOST nothing else. Later on I'll try to explain what we saw whenever we looked at Stanley and Stanley's work. If I get nothing else in this right, you have to see the Stanley we could see. Nothing in the Book of Adjectives is adequate, because Stanley is from the Book of Acts, and I have yet to figure out how to set down what is remarkable about the immeasurable.

9

Opera, Ensemble, with Gulls

Ra-awr . . . silence . . . raawr-r-r . . . silence . . . Five men in and on the hull, the only sound the snarl of Tony's drill punching screw holes in a forward bulkhead. Silence again, with gull-squawk beyond the shed, as the big scavengers flap and scroll at each other, dancing for crumbs after lunch. Dedicated meditation, decision, meter calibration, wire joinery, measurement, a cough, Billy's bucket of microballoons, a thick gray (to my red-green colorblind eyes) sludge that will harden on air-exposure to be sanded fair over minor unfairnesses in the hull surface, prior to priming and paint.

Ra-awr . . . silence . . . raawr-r-r . . . silence. Earl's approach to metalwork—dirty, noisy work that he hates so much—he makes himself do it faster, better, and louder than Lyn Smith, the steadiest man in the shop with metal.

Paul's rasping cello tone on a bad day; his easy nasal drawl, no *r*'s, no final *g*'s on the rare good day. The curious catlike hum permeating the hull when both Heliarc generators are on; the endless hushing drone with only one running; a fan pushing fire, surging slightly and falling back to the snap and hiss of Lyn's gun high in the bow, micro-volcanic, joining plate to plate, surface to surface, silver, quicksilver, silver again.

THUMP! A drill lands hard in a washbasin, drawing Earl's instant attention: Unless Tony wants to take up plumbing, he will drop his tools on the temporary cabin deck.

But Earl's voice is half a chuckle, a light machinegun sound heard muffled beyond a ridge, a mutter of metal behind it. Tony's world today is flat. Young, big, husky, quiet, good-natured, here a year before myself—just now Earl finds him suited to flatwork. That is, waterproofing with Formica the surfaces around showers, washbasins, and flushes.

His flat world is dominated by every edge that has to meet the shape of the hull, and every edge has to meet in a joint as seamless as humanly possible and lay flat to bulkhead and deckhead and hull ceiling. So every piece has to be as big as possible, then urged into precise location inside what amounts to a cramped closet occupied already by Tony, tools, plumbing, and panels already in place, on which one must NOT spatter the quick-drying panel adhesive—since noon etching everyone's lungs—but worst of all, Tony's trapped in this geometry gone berserk in a closet with only his hand and eye to make it solid.

The work of most joiners is the business of neatly coupling one straight line or edge to another. Ashore, our machines cope with most of the curves of our daily life. The straight post and rigid beam embraced us for so many hundred generations that we only lately began to dream up tools able to cut, quickly and cleanly, the curves we needed for car, boat, storage vessel, airplane, and spaceship, and precisely mark the cut-lines.

In less than a generation, the personal computer and its driver programs have been developed beyond mere design capability. Someone by now surely has a machine into which the scanning of two or three photographs of a given shape plus its known dimensions will produce plans for the replication of that shape at full scale. The hand will only prod buttons until the plans reach the shop floor. And the essential thinking is alleged to have happened before that? I'm not so sure.

We understood the Roman arch well enough to bridge most of our rivers, but the Gothic cathedral roof defeated more than one builder. Several crashed before completion, in the continuing drive for lightness and strength in structure. A few killed their architects.

If we judge by what remains of ancient historical bits and pieces, it looks as if some of the secrets that made many Greek and Roman and Norse vessels light and swift and beautiful got lost when the lights went out and had to be rediscovered along the way to what we hope is modern shipbuilding. If you understood the lines on linen or parchment or paper, and had been apprentice to men who built well, you could extend those lines with reasonable fairness, using a long flexible batten of thin wood to mark your timber. But it might or might not have been what the naval architect had drawn. Close, but we have to wonder what was lost while the naval architect increasingly over the centuries became more and more distant from the building sheds. In fact, until the later nineteenth century what came down the ways was rarely the architect's exact dimension. It was the product of creaturely skills, born of carving bowls, migrated into the shipyards in the name of those now dead in all but a few native and traditional boatbuilding sites. The name of dubber. Now a joke, the name once wore a pair of canny eyes, a pair of careful hands, could hone an adz to razor sharpness, and with it dress timber and plank to a fairness of line and curvature that would allow a hand plane to finish the clean curve. If at the end of the day the dubber drank a bit more than the rest of the yard crew, he could afford it. An expert dubber was paid more than any joiner but the foreman, whom he often replaced when that worthy retired. In the great yards of the Age of Sail, the dubbing crew circled each growing vessel constantly, each adz in effect a sculptor's chisel, fairing frames and then planking, in sections where a lot of wood had to come off quickly before the hollowing-out planes could be used.

Not the architect's but the dubber's lines went at last into the water, and it was finally the dubber's work that saw her fare well or badly on most points of sailing. We've been a long time killing the dubber and haven't quite finished him. I've read that he still lives in a few isolated pockets, legendary as the Coromandel Coast, deep and far as the Norway fjords.

Do not suppose that dealing with flat surfaces inside a boat is simple or even slightly less aggravating than creating hills and valleys in a plate or plank or frame. Tony's work, if less glamorous than anything turned out by Stanley, still had to meet every hull section exactly, and exactly meant endless repeated scribing and spiling.

Scribing and spiling are more than the nuts and bolts of shaping pieces of boat, they are the manna and hosanna of the boatbuilder's art. The two methods of measurement are closely related, and both prevent the wasting of material and time, of which no boatbuilder ever had or has enough. To scribe is to mark with a compass the line to be cut on your work-piece, and to spile is to "take off" (mark off) the outline of an irregular object by measurement from a fixed line.

BOTH of these statements are almost perfectly non-descriptive of the two procedures, but both make perfect sense as soon as you observe a joiner using them. A journeyman joiner will use what is at hand to substitute for an absent compass or a missing rule when making a rough scribe or spiling. Anything from marks on a saw blade to a long splinter snapped off at useful length. Pages and chapters have been written. You are welcome to them; they confuse me beyond hope.

In landside work, a finish carpenter (or joiner) will eventually create a *coped* joint in some household trim. I am not going to describe THAT, either. But coping, scribing and spiling are variations on the ultimate theme of making things fit each other when they are truly reluctant to do so. I will, however, simplify your life.

If you live near a coast, take a day off from your normal world and go to a boatyard where boats are built of wood. Identify yourself to the joiner foreman and plead mercy. Some will patiently show you, in less than five minutes, both scribing and spiling; others will demand some kind of payment. If the latter, show him the money and pay him AFTER you know you know. Even in boatyards, there are experts who ain't.

If you don't live near a coast, find yourself a middle-aged cabinetmaker (grumpy if possible) and broach the subject. Same rules apply. There you are, miles ahead, and all your plank ends hooded.

I cross the bridge again leaving the hull, to trim a piece in the joiner shop. Below me Earl shoulders an awkward slab of aluminum with a curious single curve and moves to the big shear, a twenty-foot-long steel scissors against the north shed wall below. Two cuts, ummchuck, ummchuck, then he moves to the big raised grid, where aluminum plate is worked. Cleating the plate down against the grid, he rings out changes on it with a deafening hammer, stares at the result a moment, un-cleats his plate, and follows me toward the joiner shop.

At the bench, my rasp and plane trim to the line; I return to the boat. My eyes water as I board. In moments, Tony is pounding once more in the forward head, trying desperately to fit the unrelenting to the unforgiving, the hard edge of reality to the surface tension of fact. The sharp, searing fire of contact cement makes all eyes run; we choke and gag and cough. Trapped in the little hell of the forward head by the speed of setting cement, Tony's steadily rising drumroll of pound and (inaudible) curse stops with a sharp *tick!* As the last veneer corner snaps in place, he staggers to the main-cabin ladder, eyes swimming, face drenched and brick-red, shirt sweat-glued to his back, his boyish mouth a short, tight line between long, gasping gulps of less-than-fresh air. Shaking his head, he "goes ashore," off the hull into the shop.

Earl has reappeared below, eyebrows raised, watching him go. He'll need Tony in a few minutes to help scribe the hull waterline and won't be able to find him anywhere in Paul's caverns and cuddies. This particular scribing needs experience and at least one quick man in the scaffold, so Stanley's age and my ignorance keep Earl from calling us.

He shrugs, lunges up the ladder and into the cabin, right behind me, pointing out two sets of tubing and a wire-cluster that will need relief in the cover-plate I've been measuring for too long—and remembers something Paul didn't in assigning me. A second plate with a strange monk's-hood must go in first. Earl wonders why am I trying to air condition the bilges?

"Ohdearohdearohdear," he sighs, kneeling to measure for the permanent cabin sole, to be laid in teak and holly. Earl, I knew by the end of my first day, is the only accurate translator of what Paul SAYS he wants into what Paul REALLY wants but never quite has time to say. Earl, I knew by the end of my first week, holds in his head the precise location and often the exact dimensions of every piece of this hull not given exclusively to machinery, wire, and plumbing.

By the end of my second week, Earl knew I was so absorbed in my hands that I never remembered my feet. Monday of my third week, I was Twinkle-toes, Twink for short. Earl never addressed me that way, except in warning or reminding and with a despairing shake of his head, so I couldn't see the quick grin.

In spite of the constant grumble, he did not tear out or more than slightly alter any piece I put in the boat. On the other hand, I did little in those first weeks that was really visible aboard the Holy Grail. You do not see a locker door unless it doesn't fit right; it is just part of where you are and what you are doing.

Tony at last rises out of the shadow of the shed floor, trudges across the clanking catwalk-almost-bridge with another cardboard flat for a template. None of us, not even Earl, can help Tony with his cupboard quandary. Only on intimate terms will it admit two bodies. I am too new to offer advice, and Earl and the others have given Tony all they can in the way of spiling and templates. If he is finally patient, he will teach himself how to match edge and surface, arc and flat, surely and quickly, with all of Stanley's precision. Almost at the hull and looking more his normal self, he finds Earl suddenly beneath him, waving him once more below. He drops his template, trots back across the jangling, dangling bridge, our bamboo and aluminum racecourse.

10

Stanley: the Doghouse Window

The slightly less-than-perfect mistress of another yachtsman's life moored at the offshore buoy one late August evening, she would become my lesson in hurrying slowly and in how to care for one's beloved. About fifty-five feet of simple splendor, we'll call her *Shohola*.

A ketch from the time Paul built his hulls in mahogany and teak, she sported a doghouse window in need of replacement. A rogue wave or perhaps the flexure normal to a wood hull had finally cracked, clear across, a single, big pane of safety glass. Her owner was not a man to take his treasure to some Jack Handy for repair. On the chance that he might want a September vacation Downeast, he had his crew run her from Manhattan to Paul Luke, while he kept doing what tycoons do

Wandelaar, port side, forward, THE doghouse window.

best. A self-disciplined man, I thought, as I helped work her alongside next morning. She held little of the cumulate clutter many yachts acquire over time. I once read a piece—Mark Twain, I think—where a brilliant feast was described as "a cut-glass dinner." *Shohola*, easing gently alongside the float, was a cut-glass yacht.

Her crew was one young man, college age, tanned, fit, alert in the eyes. We had one of those Hello conversations, where essentials are exchanged by expression rather than speech.

He: "Beautiful up here. Not as cold as I thought."

Me: "Never really cold around Boothbay. Temperate, most of the time."

He, with half a smile: "Heard it's hot, once in a while."

Me, equal smile: "Never. Windy, a little, now and then."

He, nodding toward the sheds: "Think it'll blow today? I'd hate to scrape her."

Me: "Only in my direction. I'm the new hand."

He: "Ohh—" smiling more broadly and this time not shying off the float before I can jump across with the bowline, "Thanks. See you again?"

Me: "Could be. Paul says ask you to wait on board; he'll be right down."

He: "Right. S'long."

Yankee, very professional. Both of us scared of bashing her in front of Paul. The uproar of prelaunch work had most of Paul's attention, but he never neglected an old mistress or a man who bought and kept her faithfully. We passed on the dock, he giving me a wide leeway, so I couldn't trip and send us both overside. "Twinkle-toes" was getting around.

And since it was a long hike from church to float, I was assigned to Stanley, perhaps on the notion that if I ran from joiner shop to float all day, I could not possibly injure anybody making headway on the *Wandelaar*. I never saw Stanley actually hurry, even on days when Paul was dancing on everybody's heels. But Stanley never stopped, either, and this fact, combined with the grace inherent in every line of his work, was enough to calm Paul's tendency to urge even his eldest employee to greater speed.

A landside sash is quick and simple. You can often leave it in place, knock out the remaining glass, slice out putty and points, run a bead of putty, press in new glass points, and knife in the finish putty. If you must take out the sash, shore carpentry allows the simple removal and replacement of nailed trim and cleats.

My first sight of a doghouse window in *Shohola* was impressive. It suggested one continuous piece of teak outside and one continuous piece of mahogany inside, circling the cracked pane. Make that polished mahogany. Stanley stood meditative a moment inside the immaculate saloon, then stepped forward and, to my horror, drove a wicked-looking ice pick into the gleaming wood, THUMP! with the heel of his hand.

Out popped a bung, a wood well-cap for the screw hole beneath. Closer, I could finally see minute breaks in what had looked like continuous grain surrounding the glass. Close to these breaks, I could see in a few places a grain pattern offset, suggesting more bungs. Stanley gave me his lethal weapon, gently informing me it was a scribe, not an ice pick, and said to pop all the bungs I could find in the inside coaming; we had to pull the whole thing, four straights and four corners, and try to preserve the wood as well as possible; we would need the pieces for patterns.

Stanley needed a couple more tools, but wasn't just sure where they lay, so he would go find them. If my screwdriver had a decent edge, I was to start pulling the stainless coaming bolts, but not do more until he got back. He turned and went up the cockpit ladder.

While he was gone, I did as directed, first placing a scrap of canvas on the settee beneath to catch debris, and more canvas on the cabin flooring. When Stanley returned, I was just backing a bolt out of its deep pocket in the coaming. Stanley had with him a very old and flexible putty knife, called a "thinner," and a small backsaw with no set in its tiny teeth.

Stanley squinted until he found a joint-line between two bolt holes and began to saw downward, stopping when he could feel the blade settle into elastic caulking between coaming and interior cabin wall. A further squint, and his blade sank slowly down another cut, in short, precise strokes. The straight bottom section of coaming did not move when he stopped cutting.

"We have t' cut the caulking; it hardens up after a while," Stanley murmured, picking up his super-thin putty knife and showing me how he wanted it drawn, time and again, slicing repeatedly between coaming and glass. This took some minutes, and when we were done the coaming stayed firmly in place. "Must've stripped a set of threads and re-drilled," said Stanley, his brow placid. Hunting with more care, we found an overlooked bung. This came out, and the bolt below, and still the section stuck firm.

Working this time from below, after taping cardboard to protect the cabin varnish, we knifed our way upward until at last the lower straight came free, only a little battered. "Maybe we can use this again," said Stanley. Stanley's work was meant to stay put. With all the bolts out and his saw-cuts finished, we pried and tapped for much of the morning: we tapped with pine blocks, oak blocks, and mental blocks; we pried with delicacy, cunning, wood wedges, chisels, enthusiasm, and finally brute force, breaking at last one more straight. When the whistle blew for lunch, we had the eight inside pieces out, with two straights and one corner damaged so badly we would have to make replacements. Paul was on his way to Brunswick with the pattern for the new glass. The doghouse windowpane sat smiling its fractured smile at us, still in place, but loosened.

We cruised gently up the dock while Stanley explained minimalist sculpture to me. I think it took him perhaps twenty words, a couple of sentences delivered while he revolved the offending sticks in his hands. It will take me more.

Coaming, glass-clamp and finish in one, the cross-section of each piece was that of a breaking wave tipped forward onto its leading edge, with the concavity of its curl "hardened" to a ninety-degree angle. One lip (the breaking part) fairs to the inside or outside finish, the rabbet (front wall of the wave) runs inward across substructure to the glass, and the major flat (a line drawn through the up-tilted base of the wave) supports sealant and glass.

Ninety-seven words, about as tight as I can draw them. Maybe a small indicator of why, along with all the younger hands, I jumped at every chance to work with Stanley. The economical transfer of understanding is an art and a treasure. Stanley finished his corner before I was done sawing my straights, the two of us in a ballet between bandsaw and table saw.

Back from Brunswick after lunch, Paul brought the replacement, carefully wrapped, down to the float. Meantime, I'd had a benediction nod of approval when Stanley saw my straight sections. Euphoria reigned in the cabin, as Paul came down the ladder.

Unwrapped, the new plate revealed two corners not ground by the supplier. Paul's face said, "This is not good." We sandpapered them, without reaching the desired roundness at either edge.

Stanley said the glass must be must be rounded smooth, so that stress on a sharp edge of safety plate will not start a crack across the whole plate. Paul looked on, rankled, but in the end told us to install it, taking special care to relieve the coaming so there could not be direct contact between glass and frame. Riding in a shock absorber of marine sealant, he was sure it would be all right.

Listening hard myself, I saw the crew's ears behaving like directional antennae. Paul finally started back up the pier, taking long strides. Against the light afternoon breeze, the noise level from the big shed rose dramatically. The crew produced coffee for three, watching intently while Stanley and I shaved microtome slivers from old and new coaming sections; shave and try, shave and try again. Match ends, plane and rasp, match ends again. After a long hour, all sections would tap home tight, with hairline relief back from the glass, to be filled with sealant. But Stanley had gone quiet since Paul left and wore a face close to frowning. The crew was concerned.

Wondering if I was using my plane in some way Stanley didn't favor, I asked. He said, smiling, "I'd feel bettuh 'f 'twas ground . . . but I guess it'll wuhk."

But it took more hours: the new sections were through-bored for bolting, and new threads tapped into the sub-coaming. Each piece, old and new, had to fit in a fluid, seamless line clear around before Stanley was satisfied. Never in my life had I seen this kind of patience poured into a window. Around mid afternoon, a big fisherman went by, rocking *Shohola* at the wrong moment: my tap snapped off, deep in the coaming. A reluctant trek to the machine shop: "Are y'gainin' on her, Jawn?"

"Ayeh."

Another drill-and-tap, awkwardly angled this time, the tap caressed through its work. We got the window in. I was still slicing away run-out sealant as the whistle shrieked.

The next morning a red sun flamed the steeple at East Boothbay, as I drove by, warming it pink and human. In an early fall dryness, an overlong parching of maple and oak, we might have rain in a day or so. Oncoming drivers looked cheerful. The coves, usually hidden by late summer walls of leaf and color, danced happy sparks across the windshield. At the shop, Earl's face said he'd had mead and brawn for breakfast, and when Paul appeared, he looked like cash in hand for the next five boats.

"It snapped," said *Shohola*'s crewman, stepping inside the shed. "I heard a noise about half an hour after you all left, and when I looked, it was broken." He and Paul looked evenly stricken.

We all made good speed down to the float. The Eyes were wondering what The Idiot had done (so was the Idiot), but the fires were banked for want of evidence. We examined it; nowhere did the glass touch anything but sealant. But there was the shining, treacherous line, top to bottom, away from any corner, and hard cash gone. We began to pull coaming and wipe sealant. In the plate's lower edge was an un-ground section seen by none of us the day before.

With the plate in his station wagon, Paul went up the drive spewing gravel 'til he hit pavement. Stanley and I took incredibly great pains aboard *Wandelaar* until he returned, rechecking every new coaming with a straight-edge to make sure there would be even pressure on the doghouse glass, all the way around.

When Paul returned, the plate this time had flawless, neatly rounded edges. I could imagine the exchange in Brunswick and was willing to guess that the glass cutter had a whole new attitude toward quality control—or a new job.

With Stanley, I went at it again, this time with visits on the half-hour from Paul, who had grown a renewed commitment to supervisory encouragement. Somehow, by mid afternoon we were done. This time, it held, and *Shohola* sailed next morning, glass and crew relieved.

One glass plate. Two men full-time, one man part-time. Expensive mahogany, plus a day and a half and some. I don't care what kind of custom yacht you're looking at or with what urgent longing, that thing is solid gold.

A young apprentice is a lead-pipe cinch; you can fit him into your plumbing anywhere. An old apprentice is work-hardened, probably threaded wrong. Reamed out and re-threaded, he'll still give you a conniption fit. I was fairly sure by this time that one of Paul's firm convictions was that old apprentices want regular reaming. And I misuse the word, because with Paul this took some form of encouragement toward speed and efficiency, usually delivered in a voice anxious with urgency but sometimes, just sometimes, arriving with a sarcasm suggesting that the workman brought his lunchbox but left his wits at home.

When I'd told Earl up front I'd never built boats, it was just good sense for him to regularly check up and to issue an advisory lament where he thought it would help. The exact problem lay with me, not him, because I saw myself as slower than the other joiners, especially at first. While the sound of Paul pacing across the dizzy bridge to *Wandelaar* added to my own anxiety, I began to realize in a few weeks the frequency and duration of Paul's visits to my work site were less and less. But Earl's usual proximity on board or in the shop was enough to stem any quick rise in confidence during my early months in the yard, and my novitiate soared or submerged with the rise and fall of either man's eyebrows, aimed my way.

Given a nervous grip on a genuine convention, in a few days Earl gave me a chance at a solid grab. Stanley and I have been set to work again on doghouse coaming for *Wandelaar*'s four big windows—not ports, windows.

Compared with these giant panes, *Shohola*'s window was (forgive me) a snap. These were about sixteen inches high by four feet long, per item, two on each side of the house. The interior coaming was already in, but rough where it ought to be smooth. My gloom at being allowed to shape the same cross section sixteen times was tempered only by my joy at finding the doghouse sides a wicked curve, while the glass was relentlessly straight. But Stanley's laying-on-of-hands had made a miracle. I broke no glass; I remade only two corners; I got my pair in about as quickly as Stanley set his own. This amused Stanley, alarmed Earl, and astonished Paul, who sent me off to the machine shop, while he thought about it. What better job for a man ignorant of stainless steel than the making of steel mirror-support clips?

We are still setting doghouse glass, when Stanley arrives one morning with a wretched early fall cold. Or maybe a dose of goldenrod, we don't know. He is coughing and sneezing furiously, and his eyes run so badly he can hardly see. The weather aids and abets; the heat inside the shed is over eighty degrees, and we don't want to know what it is in the hull.

Fitting the coamings means endless trips back to church, to the one really sturdy table saw we can trust for hairline trimming. And church is across the dizzy, rattling tea-garden bridge, which has developed an unreliable railing and a drunken wobble. Nobody talks about it, but Stanley's misery makes him hourly less steady on his feet. No matter, not even an outraged nose dictates to Stanley. Back and forth he goes, myself in company, when I can manage it. But I notice by noon that when I'm not at his back, one of the younger men finds something to put him within one jump, every time Stanley gets near the bridge, one after another, someone is convenient.

Not long after lunch, Stanley notices and is shortly about as grumpy as Stanley ever gets, which is not so much grump as dreadfully dignified. Finally even Earl, who gives way to no one on that bridge, somehow conjures a patient, thoughtful look, a face of modest introspection, paring moodily at a broken thumbnail, while he waits at one end or the other for Stanley to pass. This upsets Stanley so much he is out of the sheds and into Billy's car before the whistle. Stanley NEVER puts down tools before the whistle.

Next morning Stanley is himself again. The early goldenrod, he thinks. We just never talk about these things.

Boarding, Paul has a visiting family in tow, two charming daughters, young son, crisp-coifed wife, and the pleasant but booming executive voice we've heard for half an hour, inspecting this, remarking that, noting the other, questioning, questioning, questioning.

Paul likes his visitor—good face, strong character, fine intelligence, a real interest in cruising yachts. But the flood of query, by the time they board *Wandelaar*, has his eyes ridging up a little.

A thorough inspection of *Wandelaar*, during which the technology, number, and location of on-board heads become audibly impressive. "Wal," our leader is heard to mutter, " 'nuff so you wudn't hafta aim."

The family gathering in the cockpit, The Voice booms again, "Paul, you've built as many of these as any man alive, and God knows I've sailed enough of 'em. Always have trouble with the head, tried a dozen of 'em by now. Always clogged up. Tell me, d'you know of just one marine head that'll work every time? Under all conditions that you'd recommend, out of your experience, over all the rest?"

The voice stills, and echoes begin to check in from Round Pond, Bath, Biddeford and Boston. I mean, this voice in a pulpit could found a religion. Silence, finally, while Paul mulls a lifetime afflicted with obstinate oceanic plumbing.

At last, drawing a deep breath, Paul expounds. "Wa-a-al, no."

The inquisition is subdued, while the tour moves through spar shed, machine shop, and office. But the gent is chuckling, when they get into their car to leave. I would be willing to bet that my maximum leader is going to build this man's boat.

11

Foraging: the Hunter-Gatherer

Plannin' a big paahty fer th' la'nch, Paul?" A local politician is expanding his broad *a*'s in my employer's reluctant ear as I hesitate my way into the oil-steel warmth of the machine shop. The space heaters are on this morning. Outside the air is sharp, and every red leaf has an edge of cold blue. The outer sheds will be icy for another hour, but in here the warmth persuades me to unzip my jacket. I try to imagine myself invisible, hoping for a word with Big John, who understands taps and dies and apprentices.

John is young enough to remember not knowing one or two things. As I cross Paul's field of view, he shrugs, not quite ready to puncture an idle question this early in the day. " 'F I had my way," he drawls, digging through a further tray for the perfect bolt, "I wouldn't tell anybody, I'd la'nch at night 'th no one around. Nothin' but a lotta trouble." My motion intrudes, "Jawn, what you aftuh?"

"Need a tap," I say, inexactly. I need Big John's tap wrench, an ingenious tool equipped with a ratchet drive. It will save my knuckles in an awkward corner. I hold up a bolt that may be metric but is not nuttable by anything I can find in the joiner shop racks.

"Ovuh theah," he waves, "in that rack—heaven's sake why don't you ahsk instead of runnin' all ovuh."

His own search distracts him but not the politician. John squints at me across his lathe and mouths a silent "ee-leven-sixty-fourths" and wags multiple fingers above the steel ribbon arcing past his elbow from the lathe cutter-head. The politician is marching well now: if he shreds Paul's ear much longer this will be a warm spot for joiners. Big John finds an errand at the tap-and-die rack and drops his wrench in my shirt pocket, "Godsake don't lose it." He grins, shifting his cut plug to port, "Ever'thing in this place is filed under 'Where was it?' Never mind th' labels, match th' bolt . . . Heah 'tis—" The 11/64ths have migrated to the 11/32nds bin.

"Paul ever launch one at night?" I say.

This brings a big grin, "Naw-w-w, John. He hates ever'thing 'til he's got a bo't done, and then he hates ever'thing 'til he's got th' next one stahted. Nothin' in the world's fast enough. Never was. Includin' me an' Frank, and we're his sons—Godsake don't worry 'bout it; he growls at everybody. Jist ignore 'im. 'R growl back—we all do."

Not where I'd heard it, so far. "All day?" I wondered aloud.

"And then some," he demonstrates, shambling toward his lathe with glacial speed.

The heat of Paul's eye leaves my back, and the politician picks up pace as I head for *Wandelaar* in the big shed. There is a nervous edge in the pleading tone and the chatter begins to fade before the shop door can thud shut.

"You haven't got a backsaw?" Earl's face is a model of joinerly despair, and again I'm too futile for words. The little Japanese ryoba saw works to perfection in most places, but I've come to the inescapable cut that—in close trim and confined spaces—can only be made with a very thin saw cutting on the push stroke. The backsaw, properly maintained, will cut with its extreme tip. My ryoba will not, nor will my dozuki, the Japanese handsaw nearest like our Western backsaw. Either our elegant friends never cut into a stopped corner, or they never fail to plan ahead. In this case, I haven't planned ahead.

Japanese wooden-boatbuilding is said to be purely imitative, a catching up with and following of Chinese craft. While ignorant of Japan's development of wooden ships, I've read enough of their history to think that, outside their shore fishing, the men who might have built remarkable boats were literally lawed off the water for hundreds of years. Trade drives shipbuilding, and for centuries trade and other communication with the outside world was forbidden most Japanese. Under the guns of U. S. warships, they rejoined the larger seafaring world, against their will and certainly against old habit.

Apart from a few articles in *WoodenBoat* magazine, I know of no scholarly Western research into Japanese traditional wooden-boatbuilding, and I wonder what we may lose in access to their logic, if we fail to do this. Apprenticeship is a pre-feudal practice in Japan, and *ryobi* and *dozuki* are customary tools in all their woodwork, as is the back-saw with us in the West.

Bjorn Landstrom in *The Ship* has this to say:

> The Chinese junks were as a rule slender, seagoing vessels which could sail the oceans, whereas the only large Japanese junk which still existed in this century . . . was a broad, heavy and bad sailer. As to be expected it was nevertheless well built in all details by clever workmen. Here it is once again wished that some connection could be shown—this time with Rome—because the Japanese junk is a copy of the Roman merchant-man . . . in nearly all details except the rudder: the low bow with projecting stem, the high aftercastle, the through deckbeams and deck which has been widened to their extremities so that we are led to believe that the junk may at one time have had two rudders. Even the artemon [a forward mast and/or sail] is present.

As for "broad, heavy and bad sailer," I have three small old prints, one a perspective drawing of an eight-oared Japanese fishing boat, the other two of precisely the Roman-looking vessel Landstrom describes, with Buddha stationed below the helmsman's feet, in the 'tween decks, meditative, regarding the main windlass and perhaps the skipper's state of mind. The prints are beautiful, drawn in the U.S.A. (I guess) around 1900 by an M. Kellogg, and yes, that is an ugly rudder.

The fishing vessel, at about forty feet, is graceful in the way our Chesapeake skipjack is graceful, made for the purpose, and for inshore waters. Mast steps are set for main and foremast, these rigged down and lashed to the sheer strakes on either side forward when not in use. With her great sweeps—so big as to need two oarsmen each—set for pulling, she must have looked from land like a giant water bug carrying its tail angled high.

An *artemon*, by the way, is a small, square sail set high at the tip of a foremast raked so far forward that it most resembles the modern bowsprit. My own print of the Japanese junk shows no such rigging, but does provide a stout structure in the bows where such a sprit or foremast could be rigged and stayed. Small because of its location, I suspect it was used to maneuver in close quarters, rather than to help pull the ship along.

But I was thinking of saws. Pardon the detour. A saw kerf helps create a holding pattern for structure, but is not itself structure. Our traditional western handsaw, thick, heavy, pushed, makes a wide slot and much sawdust. The Japanese ryoba nokogiri, thin, light, pulled, makes little sawdust, and that powdery. For most hand-joinery cuts, the ryoba is as fast or faster, produces less waste, and is more accurate. But the Japanese have learned some sad things from us. I have two ryobi, one mail-ordered, one hand-picked. On days when my focus is poor, I can't use the mail-order saw. After years of use (it was the saw I had at Paul's), it now has a mind of its own in all but shallow cuts and will wander with a moment's inattention. A fingernail flicked against its blade makes a dull, surly sound. At some point I finally bent it, so it now cuts only waste wood.

Equipped later with a little knowledge and lots of luck, I found a rack of forty ryobi nokogiri on display—on the same day I got to meet and shake hands with James Krenov.

After a lot of flexing and narrow-eyed inspection and tone tapping, there must have been a momentary convergence of planetary force fields, because I still have that one, safely stored in the shop, which it never leaves, and on days of karmic benevolence it and I still make clean kerfs in whatever we need to, and occasional beautiful dovetails. When tapped it makes a proper celestial tone, a little mysterious.

*   *   *

Earl, Stanley, and Paul are three of the four best proofs I know in support of Jerome Bruner's Synthesis. I am NOT the fourth: On $4.00 an hour in the year of our Lord 1978, I can barely support Barbara and our aged cat, let alone Bruner's Synthesis. But between Bruner, $4.00 an hour, and occasional help from my mother, whose concern centers on her daughter-in-law (her son's lunacies by now are expected), we survive.

Bruner's Synthesis of Creativity says:

The genesis of hypotheses and creative inspirations is nonverbal cognition, first apprehended as a visual image (in the right brain), and later subjected to logic and discipline (in the left brain), a process integrated through the corpus callosum.

Well! Also, drat! Because I under-cognized verbally and mechanically, all I have is my scribble saying Bruner proposed his description of how we imagine things into life back in 1963. Fascination or the kettle boiling over kept my pen from writing down wherever it was I found Bruner. Elsewhere I scribbled *Scientific American* for September 1979 and leafed through that good gray matter until I went blind and gave up.

His synthesis proposes a description of the biology we hope is imagination and thought. Creativity, concept, feeling, flash, guesstimate, hunch, intuition, notion, perception, vision. Often without recognizable reason or experience an internal image, literally, a picture, appears, sometimes making us act before we can start to reason. Our act and following thought are close-coupled sequences of Bruner's "logic and discipline." With a strong enough image and if the wind is right, we end up with an external, visible, touchable, three- no four-dimensional image (if all things appear only in relation to time)— an outer image of what began with one electrochemical twitch across a tiny, a microscopic gap leaped without conscious effort by an invisible spark. We can't even dignify it with the name of "spark," because it isn't. But "isn't" becomes "is" on a "resting potential" of minus seventy millivolts across that twitch. And all we know is in that twitch.

Bruner began with seventy millivolts (defined with a minus sign to indicate potential across the cell membrane). All of us did, and do. The act you are now cognizing verbally in disbelief came well down the line. Minus seventy millivolts. Isn't that wonderful in this Age of Galloping Megawhops? All the interior universe we know about can twinkle along nicely at rest on a voltage that wouldn't defoliate a flea.

What little we know about the universe inside out heads includes it being a structure of one hundred billion neurons. This is an estimate, a figure I feel rather than know is somewhere in the ballpark. Nonverbal cognition, as Bruner proposes. Somebody else, dedicated, diligent and patient, has cut into a useful number of tenants of the morgue and examined, counted and multiplied results on the basis of known structure and volume, and this eases my confusion about numbers well enough that I feel it is probably about right.

These hundred billion neurons count neurons, copulate, rob banks, drive nails and points home, and form committees; they build and ruin civilizations, eat caviar and raw grubs, fry fish and murder each other, singly and in groups; they inspect ancient rock and new moons; love old bones, graceful women and gossip; pass laws and gas; hate getting up, exercise, and taxes; make music and mistakes, read entrails and journals; develop busts and philosophies, fear time and each other and have been known to cognize verbally at tiresome length on paper, as in my own case.

They do all this by communicating with each other, much of the time at levels far below their full potential. They do this with such whimsy that we have yet to figure out how they do it and scratch at the same time. And they do this for about an average seventy years on a basic power supply of seventy millivolts.

Each of these hundred billion neurons communicates through switching contacts with one, several, or many of its friends in the structure. These switches we recognize verbally as synapses, from the Greek for "unions" or "junctions," about which we and the Greeks agreed just long enough to form democracies. The probable number of synapses is around one hundred trillion, a heady number indeed. I have to cognize it verbally as the stars in more Milky Ways than I will ever find in the night sky, stuffed into a headful of micro-sparks.

The power equivalent of the micro-sparks bridging the switch points— the minus seventy millivolts internal to each resting neuron— seems a very small fry until we multiply seventy by one hundred trillion by the number of things we imagine, think, see, hear, smell, feel, and do each day. Now you know why apprentices sweat: our brains are hyperactive beyond imagining, awake or asleep.

"Experience is priceless," we say, knowing well that the toll for understanding is the time we need to get all these millivolts dancing in useful patterns—years for a lawyer, a decade for a doctor, half a life for one great page of philosophy, science, medical summation. God knows how long for anyone brave enough to try ministering to the spirit.

The spirit. The spinning jenny and Henry Ford had one great thing in common. They initiated modern-era systems demanding that the person serve the machine. The greed for gain that followed the jenny made a few rich and some noble, but it created also some of the worst industrial slums in all history, right in the heart of Merrie England. Henry Ford, whatever his opinion of history, had read enough so it persuaded him to hire bright people. First he paid a good wage, and then he tried social experiment up to and including planned communities for his workmen and their families. And some years ago I read that

Henry's company had agreed to give every line employee a personal computer as part of its current agreement with the UAW. Even in AD 2000, a relatively old corporation is willing to learn. It gives one hope.

But I came to Paul for experience, not (I hope) a mental meander. Paul cares loudly and often about both experience and time, but is famous for cruising his sheds, collecting used sandpaper, and reusing tag ends of his trove. Paul did not start out with money and reminds us of this on schedule. But after a few weeks, I want most to know how he became this magnet for talent.

One hundred billion "wires"—neurons—chemically interwoven through one hundred trillion switch points, using one-fifth of the body's chemogenesis, most of the time only to keep its support systems alive and procreating. A metabolic energy, we're told, equal to about twenty watts, day and night. The creature who goes forth to multiply, understand $E=mc^2$ and take care of things in the local galaxy is a dim bulb.

Wattage is the amount of power required; amperage is strength of current, and voltage, the potential difference, the life-giving head of water behind my dam/neuron and yours. Don't quit: we're almost back to seventy millivolts.

If wattage is stated as the product of amperes times volts, even numberless me can play in the mud hiding the lotus: 2 volts x 10 amperes = the 20 watts of my sweaty self, inexperienced; but 10 volts x 2 amperes = 20-watts-Earl, efficient, effective, and producing the same wattage, but in fact pouring out far more light with much less heat. And with less heat, more fire of creation. Oh my, yes.

But another sort of fire will be applied to this, if I neglect what Earl must often use to channel his fire—my ohms of inexperience and other-experience; my conduit-resistance to his higher voltage, still rousing the wrong fire two or three times a week. But experience and time will alter my switching pattern, my current-flow, smooth the walls of this habit-scarred conduit. My ohms of inexperience and amperes of other experience will go down, and my available voltage up, as Earl reams out my oh-my-oh-dear errors, improving my potential, setting us both to the work at hand, neatly to Earl's equation: 10V x 2A = 20W.

While I'm pretty sure after these few weeks that I'm too scarred with alien experience for anything like it to happen to me, suppose Earl worked his calculation on a very young apprentice, a clean conduit, a clean slate? We don't know a fraction of what we'd like to know. Earl is a first-rate teacher by example; when I just watch him instead of listening to his anxiety over my missteps, I get big chunks of good stuff, as several of us do watching Stanley.

But with the right apprentice, Earl might drive the amperage in the formula to an immense figure, the voltage to an awesome potential. The formula Paul plus Earl could teach a potential boatbuilding genius. Maybe even blinding light, no heat. A twenty-watt globe. Seventy millivolts times a hundred trillion futures times—take your pick. We can create it, transport it, use it, and describe its effects, but we don't know what electricity is. Seventy millivolts. Potential. We only know it communicates more than we know.

12

Evil Communications

If your foreman has faith that your modest millivolts can be better wired, your voltage will finally rise, while ohms and amperage go down. Working for Paul, I had no lack of foremen. All hands knew more than I did, and most worked with an efficiency humbling to the novice I still felt myself.

But I still had days when the ohms ran to unbelievable peaks, and the heat of frustration from my prior lack of hands-on boat work felt like terminal amps. If I reached an uneasy truce with Earl, a point where we both seemed to think I knew what I was doing, then Paul would snatch me back into purgatory with some chore alien to my practice so far.

There is a woodworking difference of opinion that probably began with the first rude shelter Adam raised after Eden stopped. It may have been part of the dispute over which Cain slew Abel. Children tend to side with one parent or the other, and it is safe to assume that the boys heard Eve tell Adam just how she wanted her lintel improved. And then Adam's reply, of course.

A few days short of September, Paul took offense at the neat innocent front of the main-cabin starboard settee. The stained-glass lockers or that morning's weather (August delight, but warm), or maybe his breakfast eggs had curdled on him. We didn't know why until much later, but the condition of the eyes at 07:00 said this would be a day of diligence for all hands.

Much of the morning I found ways to work where he wasn't, but toward noon he found me with a mirror up and my hands down. Careful to keep me in view, he herded me into *Wandelaar*'s (the *Cash Flow*'s?) saloon, beneath the gleaming doghouse window moldings.

About fourteen inches high by six feet long, the settee front, I thought, was a handsome piece of understatement, in clear flowing butternut. Its inboard length held up the seat. It neatly concealed lockers beneath hatches where the cushions would sit. It could not catch dust. No sliding foot could kick anything loose from it. I had never really examined it before, but never mind that. I was convinced it was perfect. I was careless enough to say so.

In half-inch, half-round butternut, said Paul firmly, he wanted the molding applied to that settee front. He drew his careless but silent employee a little sketch and patrolled off with his expression at medium smolder.

A short meditation convinced me that he probably wanted something a size larger than three inches of molding for this suddenly vast region, but I was more inclined to batten down than to open up and ask.

But Stanley would know; Stanley, infallible when it came to wood. I showed him the sketch. With great precision, he removed and replaced his cap and said, "Hahd t' tell just what size he wants; bettuh ahsk Earl, John."

In church I was asking Earl, when Paul materialized. Earl vanished. His sawdust devils had not settled when Paul, his face clamped shut, finished a full-scale drawing of my doom that day. "Now," he said, between clenched teeth, "theah's your pattuhn." He pointed carefully with his rule, so I could not mistake the glue-rack for his slab of cardboard. On his way out, he sighed. The dusty vinyl sheeting inside the skylights sagged in the sudden heat.

A short, noisy hunt taught me that Paul's people made any needed molding and prepared none of it in advance. If Paul saved last year's sandpaper, he was not a man to buy lumberyard molding. Lumberyard molding is made in miles, on variants of a machine called a "molder" (ugly enough) or a four-sider (which looks and sounds like two cabless Kenworths making love in a hailstorm). Lumberyard molding is the most expensive wood in the world, because the customer is buying molding, four tons of cannibal iron, a Maine farmer or MIT-trained engineer to train the molder and clean its teeth, and the tremendous waste—often fifty percent to eighty percent of beginning wood volume—made by the machine.

Small-shop moldings are made on a shaper (1/10th of a Kenworth, and be sure to wear eye, ear, and dust protection) or with a table saw and router (1/20th of a Kenworth and almost the mess of a shaper). This cuts wood waste but multiplies time, and working from rough stock adds still more time. To help matters, there was no sign of suitable shaper blade set or router-cutter. Aware that Paul's clock wore dollar signs, I started to cut twenty feet of straight stock and eyed the cutoff pile for tight-grain blocks I could use in the half-circles. Earl rematerialized with the needed router bit but stayed silent.

Paul was back twice before I had the stock planed clean but had no advice. The level of quiet from the big shed where *Wandelaar* was coming together made me think the whole crew was keeping a low profile. With Paul's mind on molding, my profile was too high and beyond help before the fragile half-circles were sanded out. I was midway through them, when Becky came by, headed for the paint shop on an errand for Billy. Becky adjusted her bandana and picked up one of the delicate bits, "What on earth are these for, John?" I had just broken one and started another.

In some heat, I mumbled, "I dunno, but maybe a four-holer for half-ass mice." Potty-trained in a less Spartan climate, Becky was nearly through her paint-shop door when my mumble registered, and she giggled. My fifth circle was near done when Earl called me to bear a hand, a fetch-and-tote assignment that shortly led to a carefully worded crisis between my boss and my foreman. As one result, they began to take turns urging me on.

Finally sure my parentheses would hang together long enough to be installed (basic test—step on them), I gathered moldings, half-circles and tools and made for the boat. Our maximum leader was present, encouraging all with pleas implying real grief at our inability to launch by 4:30. Billy glanced at me, grinning: the four-holer business had reached the boat.

"Bring th' pattuhn!" Paul's tone was level but sounded like iron about to break. I whizzed back to church and zoomed back aboard. "NO, dammit!—not th' whole THING! Cut out th' foam!"

I leaped for the joiner shop—and the only clear bench in the sheds—sliced out his half-inch-wide drawing in a white heat of super efficiency and dashed for the hull again.

Busy warming up Earl, Paul wheeled on me, "Jesus CHRIST!" he snarled, "cahn't you do ANYthin' RIGHT! You need th'—God DAMN I'll get it m' SELF."

He was halfway off the hull before I caught my breath: I smashed my tool tray down on his misbegotten settee and howled, "GOD DAMN WILL YOU SAY WHAT YOU MEAN!"

Well. The earth froze. I managed to shut my mouth. The firing squad principle, you know, try to go down dignified. Idiots do this especially well. And yes, the futility of my existence flashed by in one great eternal blink. For two seconds the world could hear the parson's cat fart in Port Clyde.

One. Two. Squeak-CRASH! Life resumed, as Paul steamed across the bridge away from the hull. I had a fist and my resignation clenched, when he stormed back on board, slammed himself shoulder-down on the cabin sole, and tacked the inside of his pattern to the settee front. Providing a neat edge around which the molding could be tacked in near-zero time. The hull, I suddenly noticed, held no life but us.

"Theah," rising, he sighed gently.

Full of self-loathing, stupidity and general anguish, I couldn't match Earl's talent for vanishment. I mumbled some kind of mea culpa and apology, while he brushed off his shirt. "Now," he explained, just loud enough to shut me up, in a tone mild as the afternoon breeze, "is that simple enough?"

I still could not move. But he seemed to read something useful in whatever he saw; cocking one brow, he straightened his cap and patrolled light-footed off the hull. I drove the last brads with the afternoon whistle.

Heat, hurry, confusion, frustration. He supposed and I assumed— in a situation where too often communication is a four-letter word. I trucked all my tools back to my chest in church, thinking he might have changed his mind. He hadn't. Outside in the parking lot, he stood talking with the reason for my afternoon disaster, Mr. and Mrs. Owner.

A half-hour later, after consulting with Barbara and Goodness and Mercy, I picked up the kitchen phone. Barbara had a doctor to see, and Red Rover, between shop and apartment, had settled on second gear after disposing of third and toying with park. I'd sooner have picked up a live grenade than the phone.

"Puhfectly all right," he drawled, "no problem. These things happen . . . I'd appreciate it 'f you'd come in soon's you could, though—lotta wuhk t' do . . . Thanks f' callin'."

Shaking my head, I packed up Barbara and the cat and headed north in second-gear shock. My boss had barely a nod out of me leaving the sheds, still shaking as I was with frustration. I had not really apologized to him. I would have fired me forthwith. I didn't have the skill or speed he plainly needed. He knew it and I knew it.

But I still admired what he did and wanted still to learn, and he knew that, too. And was willing for me to try. And this and that, and wouldn't we all be better off speaking only with eyes and hands.

It was one of those eerie, soft evenings, with the river gray silk skirting the road. The cat not only did not throw up his customary three times, he didn't throw up at all. He curled up in Barbara's lap, twitching a little, and dreamed old innocence. "Eerie," I said. The road, most of it a primary highway and routinely busy, was empty but for our second-gear howl through its river fields and maple arches, maroon-shadowed in the last light. Barbara dozed, the cat slept; after a while my ear adjusted to the high-tension whine from the gearbox, and even that became a stillness. Dumb and blank as an empty page, I sat while the road and the river unrolled ahead and vanished around me to nothing, and silence.

The following Friday night I was home and about to shower, when I found my paycheck fatter by a quarter-an-hour.

So. With Paul's token in hand, I learned to speed with moderation; I learned to keep my temper tamped, my mouth shut; I became that model of permanent apprenticehood, a possible journeyman. Earl finally dropped his guard; Paul turned into a reflective, a philosophic master; we all got on with the building of wonderful boats.

The hell we did. Well, if I thought I couldn't reach a means of measuring up to their speed and skills, why stay? Glad you asked. Before I met Paul, I'd spent odd, even, and endless hours puttering with wood. I could carve a pencil holder for hours, plane at a breadboard for a day (to little effect), and in many other ways (not in the least like James Krenov) waste time with wood. I could make stuff, but certainly not in a way that even suggested planning or efficiency.

After three weeks with Earl, I could design in my head, collect the right lumber for, and in one weekend build a radial saw table that one man could break down and tote between jobs. At the time I had a circular saw, a handsaw, screwdrivers and a couple of chisels and had just discovered the joy of driving screws with a power drill. The saw was up and working in two days with no loss of meals or sleep. So I had learned more about how to work in three weeks than I had learned since I left high school and the farm, years before.

13

Steve, Apprentice, Journeyman

We are in the wire shop, lunch buckets open, coffee in hand. Asked how he found Paul Luke, Steve tells this story:

Well, I saw this ad in the paper, you know. So I answered it. I didn't have a typewriter, so I took it over to my girlfriend's house, and she typed it up for me. I never thought I'd get the job. Jeez, I was too young, and the longest I'd worked on a boat before was a month one summer. Without pay.

I went crazy when he—after he called. Ran around in circles yelling. Never had an employment interview in my life. I couldn't believe it. Everybody tells you do this, do that, you know. And you don't know what to do, anyway. I had to take a leak something terrible the whole time. And I'd been sitting there with shoe polish on my ear, talking, but I got his letter back a couple weeks later. I got the job.

My God, a hundred a week, live aboard, all my food. I was sixteen and rich. Ran all the way over to my girlfriend's house to show her. The interview? Scared to death; I'd been in Manhattan a dozen times, I guess, shopping, with my parents, a movie y'know, stuff like that. Jeez, this guy designed ships for the Navy, flew all over, had his own jet, everything. Great big office with a huge room full of draftsmen. I remember the outer office, mostly. His office had a big window-wall, looking toward the river, whole bunch of secretaries. The one that took me in was wearing white slacks. Followed her down about a mile of plush hallway y'know. They were a little tight. By the time we got there, I was brick red. She thought it was pretty funny.

So he asked me some questions. I dunno. School, sports, what kind of work I'd done before, summers. School. Grades. All I could say at first was yes or no. Jesus, I was all screwed up. That girl y'know. I dunno if I said one whole sentence the whole time he talked to me. But I guess it was all right. He showed me around after we got done talking. I was still shook up and had to pee so bad I couldn't see anything but the men's room.

So my girlfriend borrowed her mother's car, and we ran right down to see the boat. He sent a note with the letter, so I could go aboard, get some idea of the layout and the work. I never saw so much teak in my life.

Well, she might have been taken off a Herreshoff design, made bigger. Beautiful bow, nice clean run aft, into a counter stern. Beautiful. I mean, *everything!* The layout was designed for his family; they had a little boy and a girl. Crew berth was way forward, but it wasn't bare, like a lot of 'em. Thick, comfortable mattress, plenty of blankets, place you could plug in a razor, a mirror, plenty of light. I like to read, and it was a nice place to read any kind of weather, unless you had a really bad head sea. Lots of locker space, finished pretty much like the main cabin. I dunno. I've always been crazy about sailing, and this was—she was just about the prettiest ketch I ever saw. It just felt good walking around on her deck, knowing I'd be sailing her, probably two or three seasons.

I was still checking sail bags, when he got there after work. And then I found out how much work I was looking at. It turned out—well, I liked him all right, but I mean he was meticulous, I guess is the word, very, very careful about everything. Everything just so. He had schedules and lists, and lists for his lists. Jeez, I still remember those lists. He had a new one every week, sometimes twice a week. No scratch ever got through two days on that boat—sanded down and varnished, painted, right away, no ifs or buts. Th' cabin sole came up, and the bilges got wiped down, at least every second day.

Now I remember why I still hate lists. I'd been working then a month, six weeks I guess, and we got back after a couple weeks cruise, Downeast. Came back down the Sound that afternoon;

it was pretty wet but not so bad we couldn't keep sail on her. Anyway, he left his usual list—cleaning, paint, varnish, sails, turn the halyards. Got the family packed into the car; his wife was really nice, I thought; she gave me a present for Millie, just as they were getting into the car. For keeping her lonesome so long, she said.

So they took off, and I was drying sails before I stowed 'em. And then I wanted to call Millie to tell her I'd be over, you know, so I just dumped the sails and hiked up the pier, around the building to the phone.

And there was this guy talking, jeez he went on and on. I circled around him, and he kept on talking. I looked at my watch, and he kept on talking. And I wanted to get back, get sail stowed and the boat cleaned up, get outa there. I was just about to go back to th' boat, when he finally hung up, said he was sorry, and took off. So I called, and she took a while getting to the phone, and I guess we talked a few minutes before . . . well, I hung up.

I ran back to the boat, and there was the car and the family and his wife looking worried, and there he was in the cabin, writing lists. One right after another. "You might as well know your job is in question," he said. And I started to tell him about the phone, and he wouldn't let me. "I don't want to hear excuses," he said. "Our rule was the boat first, and then your time's your own. No excuses," he said, "we agreed to it."

He didn't yell or anything; he was just mad, and he wouldn't let me say anything. "Get the sails packed up," he said, like I wasn't anybody, not looking at me. "I don't want to hear about it. I trusted you, Steve."

So I got busy with the sails. By the time he was done, he had a list ran more than three pages. I couldn't believe it. Picky crap, one cup hook, towel hook, I mean, loose, that kind of thing. Locker catch rattling, a wipe rag left in the engine compartment. And the rest of it stuff he could see I was doing anyway, every day. Wrong, I guess, but not the kind of wrong he cared about.

He shoved the list across the table at me and stood up and started up the ladder. "I'll let you know tomorrow afternoon about your job," he said, not looking at me. "I'm really disappointed in you." And he turned, just walked off then, before I could say anything. I followed him up the ladder, I guess; I don't remember.

By the time he got to the pier steps, up from the float, you know, I was mad. I guess I was crying a little. I couldn't see very well. I just couldn't believe it, and I yelled at him, "IT'S NOT FAIR." You know, a dumb kid yelling at an angry man, what good does it do, "IT'S NOT FAIR IF YOU WON'T LET ME SAY ANYTHING. DAMMIT YOU'RE NOT BEING FAIR."

And he stopped, and I stopped yelling. Then he shook his head and called back, "I'll call you tomorrow." And got in the car and went. So I worked all night and finished up next morning. Sails, trash, cleaning, varnishing—he wasn't going to have a damn thing to complain about, whether he fired me or not. I got done and took a couple hours to see Millie—the hell with it you know, I was done, I thought. And got back to the boat mid afternoon, before he got there from work.

I was tired out, and I guess he was too, when he got there. Looked that way. He looked at her. He didn't say much, at first. I'd worked my ass off all night. She was spotless. So he sat down finally, like he didn't want to. Said he was ready to listen to me, that he realized maybe he was wrong yesterday. So I told him I only left the boat open while I went to the phone. And the guy talking and all. And the man at the dock office saw me up there, if he wanted to check.

I guess it's the first time he really talked to me like a human being. Said he guessed he wasn't fair, not giving me a chance, and he was just tired and blew up when he got back to pick up the light he forgot and found me gone. It was just finding the boat open—everything in a mess you know. He'd talked it over with his wife, and she thought he was wrong, and he guessed his kids thought he was wrong, too, and if I'd let him apologize, then they all wanted me to stay with the boat. The way he said it, it sounded like awful hard work, like he wasn't used to apologizing for much, not even to his family.

But he said he was sorry, and he was pleased with everything else so far, the way it was working out. And after that we got along all right, even the next summer, when I misjudged a tide and took her masts out under a bridge. I figured I'd really done it that time. But I called him right away, and he said it was all

right, it was covered, he understood how it could happen that
way just at twilight, and don't worry about it.

I said, "But how'd you come here, Steve?"

"Paul built her. I've got some pictures at home. I wish you could
see her. She's a beauty."

The one o'clock whistle blew. We went back to building all the
stuff Steve fell in love with at age sixteen. Actually, he was late. My
grandmother always insisted I tried to stow away on a New Bedford
dragger when I was five. All I remember is a startled and then angry
Portuguese fisherman yelling at me to get off his boat. I know he just
didn't want to have to explain a drowned kid. But while I remember
only that he was big and dark and upset, I can still draw you a picture
of his boat.

14

The Royal Flush
(or the 120-Volt Necessary)

The family car these days is less apt to shower sparks and the rich perfume of burnt insulation. I have vivid memories of one car that did burst into flame with some regularity. It was a '38 Chevrolet Knucklehead coupe, named in honor, I'm sure, of its engineers, buyers and drivers. I was innocent of its design—and much else—when I bought it, but within a week or so had a firm grip on its principles and several wrenches acquired in haste.

That alleged vehicle and most since carry something called a "wire net," designed over man-years of careful drafting. This net is assembled from precut lengths, in one plant, and is finally inserted in a car in a different production line by specialists, who know its junctions so well they could plug them in blindfold. The work is scheduled, checked and rechecked, but the system fails here and there. One or another of us, seeing the repair bill, can never again believe the blindfold isn't a fixture.

When you want an engine at sea or in harbor, you want it *now*. We like to forget the gripping sphincter and fear-sweat of finding a fixed or moving object bearing dead on and far too close, but there are equal evils on the water. A dead switch or lamp at home is most often an inconvenience. At sea, it can be deadly. If your car is ill assembled, you're not likely to find it melting around you as a result of leaking or poorly grounded voltage. Not so the boat, whether it has a wood or metal hull. All voltage in every circuit must be accounted for, down to the last quiver of voltmeter, preferably before launch, since a bad fugitive ground can unfasten a plank or dissolve a through-hull fitting in alarmingly short order. It happens, but I've yet to hear of it happening in a hull built by Paul or his peers.

We all love convenience, but too many of us are bored with some of the inchworm details of creating convenience. I was, until I came to understand more about *Wandelaar*, "Royal Redundant." She carried two huge sets of marine batteries. The first pair served as starting power for the big diesel auxiliary, which drove her self-feathering propeller. The first pair also could be switched to crank her 120V generator and further switched into emergency power for her 12V lighting and instruments. The second pair supplied normal 12V power through the boat.

All batteries were normally charged by the big alternator belted to her auxiliary but could also be charged by a completely separate diesel-electric generator, also switched to provide either 120V or 12V and also buried in the engine room, across from a compact distilling plant designed to turn saltwater into fresh. This item hardly looked like a fair substitute for what's usually a mile up a Kentucky hollow, but I managed to keep still about my ignorance of modern alchemy.

The remaining mysteries under the main-cabin sole lay in tankage, wiring, plumbing, terminal blocks, and small switchboards, and among these often lay Bill-the-Wire chanting Hail Marys toward the hope that her owner held advanced degrees in all things electric. The passage wall between the saloon and owner's cabin held two switch-and-dial panels. Their sheer number and variety made me count them. As with much else I did while working for Paul, this was interrupted. But before I lost track, I ticked off over sixty units, gauges, breakers, and switches, each neatly lettered to tell function. The tiny blocks usually said "Running Lgts" or "Galley Lgts, Pt," which made sense even to my low voltage, but some of the main breakers wore strong, dense language, pointing to Fate and the Furies if one threw any of several combinations in the wrong order. As far as the joiners were concerned, these could never cause harm: none of us would willingly have touched one. The reason was honest enough. None of us, up to and including Paul, knew from one week to the next what in hell Bill and Steve were doing. As a matter of form, Paul would come by and scorch them, lightly and in exact measure, most mornings: "What on earth's THAT?" he prodded, viewing with alarm.

"Oh, this?" Bill said, without looking up. "A bipolar reversible culpitor with an override paranoid."

Or Steve, head in locker, "Semble, FRAMjerbilsh—" Steve was raised with precision in mind, and former gurus could only have reinforced this, but it was hard to tell with his head in a hole. In either case, Paul's instant response was, "You put them in LAST week, dammit!"

Which brought the calm, clear reply, "One didn't work."

With a sigh, Paul would resume patrol toward his next target of opportunity, refreshed and ready to smoke out some carelessness he could deal with.

If any joiner but Earl moved within reach of those consoles, or had to work in the engine room below, he found himself under the anxious eye of Steve or Bill and at least once a day was prayed at: "Watch where you drill, now, Jeez, I don't need neon eyeballs." Or, "Hey! Carefuldammit! Doing this once is enough!"

From the big boards, a double net fed the boat, one net 12V and the other shore-side standard 120V. Switched properly, the latter net could be plugged into U.S. shore outlets, into foreign voltages through accessory plugs and transformers, and to the vessel's own generator. Switched wrong, you could buy a silver dinghy with the cost of repair.

Several cable clusters in the engine room and back of the consoles began as thick as your wrist, and all nerve trunks, from source to outlet, ran close to interior surface finish. Installing the wire demanded every flexion painful to the body: Steve and Bill hung head down, twisted trunk, head and arms inside lockers, craned at length across hard-edge joinery and machinery, disappeared for whole mornings inside drawers I didn't think could hold a child, sprained everything from the hips up at least once apiece, gashed hands continually on edges and wire no crew would ever see or touch again, worked wire through cuddies so cramped that one had to push the other in and later haul him out, and almost never swore, although some of the wire lay in places where a careless drill cost them a day of torture later. That there were few misaligned drill holes and only one mistake with a sharp-edge wire mesh used to retain engine-noise-damping insulation speaks well for the joiner crew's attention to detail. When *Wandelaar* settled on her launch truck in October, she had been eighteen months building.

By the time we were done with cabinets, doors, hatches, molding and grab rails, all joiners and both wire men had nervous tics. The electric tendrils ran to the anchor winch, to about a dozen pumps (including the four flushes plus treatment/holding tanks), to the freshwater

Owner's cabin, bunks and storage.

distiller, to an air-conditioning-climate-control system throughout the hull, to winches for sail handling, a tape deck/audio system with stereo speakers in all cabins, two radio transceivers, Loran, sonar, radio direction finder and radar, to an autopilot lurking in the lazarette (compartment for storage and steering equipment in the stern) to running lights, crosstrees deck lights, cabin lighting, instruments AND, for when the crew finished with any of three electrically pumped showers, the dumfounding (to me) luxury of clean, dry clothing from a full-size domestic washer hidden in the owner's cabin, plus an electric dryer shoehorned behind a saloon settee/bunk. I'd seen landlocked mansions with less plumbing. And I had to examine this owner's multi-button, mega-pipe magnificence twice—I wasn't sure the first time that a bidet wouldn't spring to plastic bloom at the touch of a fingertip. But if there were taps in the galley for Remy Martin or Mumm's, I never found them.

The plumbing amounted to a work of art. The flushes operated by fingertip solenoid, by foot switch, and by the more traditional joystick, rising perilously close, of course, to where you sat. Marine tradition dies hard. The only thing overlooked was telekinetic wiping and flushing, but naval architecture has its limits. The royal flushes blended in four separate mixmasters, composted with chemicals, held with shushing dignity, and pumped over-side in privacy.

I may be paying undue attention here to sanitation and ought to explain. Compelled at a tender age to visit an over-ventilated arctic outhouse, I have since been a strictly utilitarian crapper, meditative only in steaming hot showers. There is no help for me: on board or ashore, a head is something needful, to be used and launched from at speed. Washroom heaven, on the other hand, is a needle-blast shower from an infinite hot tank, with a drink convenient and all the Bach you can blow in my ear.

I've detailed this web of nerve and electric bowel only to explain why, well before all this hygiene mooned off down the bay, Bill began to resemble a positive image of the Shroud of Turin and Steve a penitent just off an Inquisition rack. To the joiners, their speech was impenetrable, their thousand-yard stares reached two thousand yards;

Wandelaar main cabin "laundry door," with AC vent, washer and dryer within.

they could confuse me, if not the others, simply by standing up, dripping wire. Their schematics, diagrams, photographs, instruction and repair manuals filled two three-inch-thick notebooks. Bill tried to make all this clear to the owner, later, while that necessary man was preoccupied with fitting-out and provisioning. Before those final weeks were done, Bill and the owner were exchanging guarded looks of mutual disbelief. And after Bill had done his best, the owner still could be found in contemplation of the control panels, his face—a face that organized industry, that played poker with international banks—verily, his face was a portrait of mystic and fugitive hope.

15

Fitting In

Grab on. Hold this. Bear a hand here. Now, pull!"

With the root of our name in the living/dead Latin "to grasp," it's no wonder Tony and I are interchangeable, vise and vice, to Earl and Stanley. Why does it take me so long to be simple? If we're gripping a work-piece Earl is conjuring, we get a rare chance—if it's not slipping—a chance to *really* watch what our foreman does, and how he does it.

On any day we are dunnage, foundation, haulage, blocking, wrenches, bench stops, wheels, pivots, levers, wedges, brakes, the workbench, and the work itself. Often there is enough of this to leave us speechless and exhausted by day's end, with little of our morning assignment done.

But this repetition of simple acts, performed long enough, will give us the grip we need on the sweaty handle of apprenticeship. This is one of the oldest practiced arts of humankind, and Tony and I are here for one purpose—to "take hold of it." Paul, Earl, and Stanley direct our taking hold, from some place miles and light years beyond books. Tony, bigger, stronger, younger, longer at this work, makes a better vise. We are clamped to a big panel and pattern Earl is marking, because we are closer than the clamps he would otherwise use. Tony doesn't catch the flick of Earl's voice so often. He seems to watch and absorb almost without effort, although I know, since the grief the veneer gave him, that this isn't always so. But he does pick it up faster, with less experience, some days with an ease that makes me mourn my misspent youth. I have much to unlearn.

Earl catches me musing and informs me sharply that he will do my thinking for me, and will I kindly get a better grip?

Maybe. Eventually. I try, in present time, and Earl concentrates once more on his pencil and scribe. The entire shape these points mark lives in Earl's mind, lifted from the plans in the office. My shift of grip, if careless, will change not only his marks but his perception of them and finally in some measure the character of the finished hull and accommodation.

We call it the "practice of law," the "practice of medicine," because we get good at it only by faithful practice over long years. Also why we admire, sometimes envy, the genius who seems not to have the learning griefs that make the rest of us stumble on our way to practice.

"HeyHEY!" Chuckling aloud and trying to glare, Earl wakes me: "Jesusjesus, take that down an' cut it will you?" Shaking his head, he knees another slab of three-quarter ply up onto the glue-frame and bends to his marks. Always furious at delay, my woolgathering this time has nearly cracked him up. Earl knows about apprentices. He is one. He has no need for the word. He is one.

16

Conventions

Paul leans over the lockers inside the primly upholstered starboard settee, pointing as he speaks, "Need inspection plates, heuh 'nd heuh, ovuh the fuel tank gauges. Same thing, th' portside tanks and why didn't the plates go in before the—uh-uh, stop right there," pointing. "Big enough so's you can see the gauges." He looks up warningly, "Plexiglas is up in th' shop. Tony knows where 'tis."

He glances up, probably with our last seminar in mind, "Any questions?"

"Nope."

Poverty, chastity, obedience, and do it; I'm your man, Paul. Besides, after the crystal locker and that molding, four buried inspection ports ought to be simple enough. Paul nods and patrols off the hull. I locate the gauges below, punch center marks, and pull the locker bottoms, four plywood plates, about forty screws, then lope off to the joiner shop. Earl, untroubled this morning by Tony, myself, or our maximum leader, is working up butternut for what will become the saloon table. The table saw wears a cardboard sign, DO NOT USE, made with Earl's marker pen. He frowns and shakes his head as I move past the thickness planer, but this time I need only the bandsaw and router. Rummaging the cutoff box beyond the table saw, I find the bits of transparent acrylic I'd noticed a few days before, gleaming back at me.

In a half-hour the little plates are nested in rabbets in the locker bottoms, and two of the four are screwed in. Looking up, I find Earl eyeing me. Oh god, what now.

"F'r th' fuel gauges—" he says, stating, not guessing, but with what could be a half-smile.

"Yeah, what?"

"Too big," he says, shaking his head. "Always make 'em about two inches, no bigger'n the gauge; use th' circle cutter on the drill press; it's faster and cheaper. Be able t' see through those all right."

Now there's a real smile. The little plates are cut about four inches by six inches.

"I could refit ply and—"

"No," he sighs, "too near done. Finish 'em up," he says, turning to his bench, then swinging back, "You took 'em outa scrap stock?"

"Yeah."

He nods, picking up his plane, leaning into it as his hand strikes the grip, pickup and glide with one smooth motion.

With gauges six inches below an already dim locker, I'd cut rectangles big enough to admit a flashlight beam while its bearer could see alongside comfortably, without squinting. One should be able to see easily through an inspection port, right? But in Paul's eyes the result would be a curtain-wall of Plexiglas, three-quarters of it wasted. And Earl would get nicked for the way they were done.

Earl's handsome saloon table, pièce de résistance.

I picked out my dullest screwdriver and marched out to the machine shop grinder, not far from the welding bench—and Paul. Every man in the place knew the edge on his neighbor's tools. The third section of locker sole was going in when he hove aboard. Paul sighed, gazing at the bilgy vistas of gauge, tube, tank, and hull offered by my gleaming portals, "My, that's wonduhful, Jawn. Where'd yuh learn t' make inspection po'ts like that?"

"Never made any before," I said, before looking up.

Stanley, checking dimensions at the main cabin gangway, gave me a long, reflective look and dissolved from sight. Paul's jaw was knotted, "Well, why on earth didn't you, didn't y' ahsk Earl, f'r cryin' out loud?"

"They were near done when he saw 'em."

The brows went up. Maybe I *was* getting faster. "He said always do 'em in small circles. From now on."

"We're nevuh goin' t' make any money round heah 'f you waste material like that. Don't need t' be any bigguh 'n the gauge itself."

"Want 'em changed?"

"NO! Wasted enough time on 'em. Trim th' after cabin drawuhs so they slide free, soon's y'r done heuh. Then come see me in the spar shed."

* * *

Earl is having a good day, judging by progress on his table. So is the middle-aged apprentice.

Earl's tawny, hand-planed planks of butternut begin to form pieces of saloon table, this one a twin-aileron, double-elevator delight that, when assembled, is far more graceful than the architect's drawing. A form clean, linear, solid and soft at one and the same time. Earl's judgment in dimension and grain-graphics make it a small monument to joinery, a table we'd like to sit down at and take our ease by.

What galls is that he made this in little more than a week, while strengthening *Wandelaar*'s launch cradle, supervising the extraction of months of building debris from under and around her, and repeatedly checking the mountain of fugitive detail that must be in place before she can move one inch toward water. Steve and Tony can be seen detouring through the paint shop, where Becky applies varnish to the table's parts—and again at noon after they finish their sandwiches.

With three weeks and absolutely no interruptions, I might make

something close to this table but not, I think, as good. While Steve and
Tony and Becky circle the altar, I have been making a small box to very
specific requirements. With the owner's cabin drawers eased, I'd of
course marched myself to Paul's welding bench in the spar shed. Using
a TIG welding unit (the electric arc is struck inside a surrounding
column of tungsten inert gas, delivered from a tank through hose to
the welding gun), he is welding rigging cleats to their pads. If the sheer
volume of sparks, stray gobs of aluminum, and his facial expression
can be trusted, his mind is miles from his bench, or the torch has
developed a mind of its own. He sets it down, removes his welding
mask, briefly thinks about turning off the Heliarc generator, and leads
me back to *Wandelaar* and the owner's head. I've described parts of the
Royal Flush.

We find Earl adding another piece, a sturdy brass door hook, so
nobody later will accidentally brain a thinker or neuter a peer. While
Earl drills and applies screws, Paul waves at the bulkhead above the
gleaming sink. The Full House, he has decided, wanted one more jewel
to perfect its glamour.

"A narrow medicine cabinet," he concludes, "the width of the
mirruh, 'bout five inches tall. It cahn't stick out ovuh th' sink heuh,
more'n four inches. No back; the wall'll take care 'f it. Brace th'
connuhs."

"What kind of door?"

"Oh-h-h, not much room. Slidin' doah, I guess. Try it an' see."

Too often when I tried it somebody saw red. I can't tell if he has
said this in hope or resignation: The Face is in better adjustment now,
and the phone hasn't rung yet. Off he goes.

Well—grinning to myself—a whole box, next to the best seat in the
house. But all the space allowed is, in effect, a skinny square pipe, four
by five by thirty inches across, between the mirror bottom and the sink
faucets. Not much knuckle room, unless I use thin stock.

Back in church I find a swirl-grain cutoff of butternut and re-
saw it on the bandsaw. Re-sawing is the process of making two thin
planks out of one thick one. You make sure one plank edge is at ninety
degrees to its broad side, draw a line halving the opposite edge for its
full length, stand the piece on edge, and let the bandsaw do its work.
The result opens like a book, giving you two leaves with mirror-image
graining and very little waste.

I shut down the bandsaw and find Tony watching wide-eyed and beyond him Earl with both eyebrows on full alert, but no frown to match. In a few years, an OSHA inspector would sound off in full punitive voice before I hit the off switch. Our Occupational Safety and Health Administration does save lives but in many ways also forbids practical simple methods of work. I should note that before I free-handed that stick through the saw, I knew the blade tension and sharpness and earlier that morning had checked to see if the table was square with the blade.

"Jeez," says Tony, "we never do that here."

"Tony," says Earl, "go help clear under th' stern." A clash of scaffolding, punctuated with the thud of shoring timber and clarion calls of urgent management has gained volume in the distance.

Top, bottom, and sides are clean, dimensioned, and about to be glued, when Management returns: "Not glued up?"

"Gainin' on it."

"Put some nails in that thing an' get it done."

I stare at Paul amazed, but he's already thinking about something else. I already know that the smallest finish nail in the shop will split these 5/16 inch panels if I don't drill them first, and without glue the case will collapse the first time it's leaned on. One well-reasoned convention of boatbuilding is "They will lean on it," whether or not a crewmember is hurled against it in a seaway, so it better be sturdy.

Paul stops, makes a 360 visual search in one spin, and vanishes again. I am fussing with clamps and dropping more than one, when Earl says something I misinterpret. A query later brings, "Don't want t' getintha middlovit, John, you go see him."

I can't blame him; Paul is growling at all in his path and is back in minutes to rankle Earl again. I measure diagonals to be sure the box is square and begin to set pins, then hear what Earl was trying to say over the din: The top of my box needs a gallery railing, or anything set there will fall off. I ponder this and ask Earl again. He just shakes his head. I recheck dimension on existing shelf railing on the boat—entirely out of scale with my box—and take a very long time finding Paul, while I yearn for the noon whistle.

Other than Frank and John at their lathes, the shop is quiet. Big John grins and thumbs me toward the spar shed, walking his fingers tiptoe across the lathe gearbox.

With his helmet flipped up, Paul's eyes are angry, his voice not. He nods agreement, "Scale it down, then, shaper blades're in the box b'neath the motuh." His jaw taut again, he turns back to his own troubles. There are lumps in the bead he's laying, and Paul doesn't lump a weld he's focused on. SPLAT! SPLUT-T-TT! The arc bounces, and Frank finds the whistle.

Over lunch I hear the reason for the upset. It seems Paul got a midmorning call from the architect. Expecting a launch weight of sixty thousand pounds, he is now looking at close to seventy-five thousand pounds. The yard's track, truck and windlass were built in a year when such things were meant to last two or three generations and look substantial. But they are aging all the same, and the wire shop guesses are pretty sure the rig has not launched anything within twenty thousand pounds of this hull. Billy warms to his subject, beginning with, "Th' lahst stawm took th' dock out 'n blew it a mile up the bay! May've spread th' rails. The launch truck had broken once. The cable snapped one time and needed a week's fishing to haul the truck back onto the railway. Got some good lobster while we looked, though. Oh, yes, three, four pots, I guess the storm dragged them inshore. And one hull fell right off the cradle, Godsake, whopped a two-foot ding in 'er."

"Well, how'd you straighten her out, Billy?" I ask.

"Oh-h-h, easy. Earl took a top maul to 'er. Popped right out just like a frypan. Solid as could be; couldn't see where th' ding was, even. Paul usually handles the whole thing . . . now . . ."

"Whaddya mean now, Billy?" I say.

"Well, f'r a while there he used t' turn th' windlass over to somebody else, now 'n then. One o' the boys, usually."

"Frank or John, you mean?"

"Ayeh. Well, we were launchin' midmornin' once. An' they got the champagne on her good—fuhst lick—an' in she went, nice's could be. But then I heuh somebody yellin', y'know, an' I begin t' look around. An' my wuhd, theah's Paul neck deep on the cradle out theah, yellin' like hell f'r one of us t' come get 'im. So I ran got the dinghy, course, and went ahfter 'im. I thought I was seein' things, my wuhd wasn't he hot! Could hahdly talk to 'im f'r a week."

"What'd he say, Billy?" I ask.

"Well he carried on some 'til he saw th' dinghy. Got 'im aboahd all right, but then he jest set theah drippin'. My he looked ugly. I had all I c'd do t' keep m' face straight, but I managed. Got 'im to th' float 'n he mahched up t'th' house, lookin' straight ahead, y'know. Changed 'is clothes, 'n come right back t' the pahty. But my wuhd you wanta get killed, you go neah thet windlass on la'nch day."

"Naw, Billy, you gotta be stretchin' it some."

"Nosuh. You ahsk Lyn, he saw it. He'll be heah f' t' la'nch, he'll tell yuh. You're wuhkin' f' the only man in Boothbay managed t' la'nch 'imself. Honest."

It's a cheerful lunch. I take my rail sections and a bit of leftover full-size rail to Paul for a glance and a nod. I set the rail aside while I try fitting slides and doors to my square banana. The little box is not going to hold much anyway, once it is braced inside, and the sliders eat up much of its front. I slice the butternut doorplates, and one snaps when I bend it even slightly. Unlike walnut, thin butternut won't take much shock. My second visit convinces Paul, who finally says to hinge them from the bottom, using piano hinge stock I will find in storage back of the wire room. And damn quick PLEASE he snaps at my heels. His tone this time holds more frustration than urgency, and I get no sense of directed anger.

But it takes time to find the hinge and screws that have to be clipped and filed. I have another piece of butternut clean and bored for finger-holes, when Becky comes by, curious to know why I'm leaving skid marks between church and the spar shed, and "Hey, what's that cute box with the holes in the front of it?"

"A two-unit mouse house, honey." She loves it, and Earl has to turn his face away for a minute. The world improves, but it takes a focused hour to get the doors rabbeted, trimmed, hinged, and press-fitted to the case. At the whistle, I set the piece at my end of the long bench, in case the Night Patrol comes by, and leave before the leader of us all can comment.

Next morning, Paul's cutting edge is gone, but again I'm first in line for the morning paper, by the sound of it about number eighty grit, "Admire th' fit o' those doors, but ye'll nevuh close th' damn things wet."

I take a deep breath and say that by setting my doors before relieving for clearance, I need only one trim to exact marks all around. I say this quietly, but I am tired of drawing fire and about done with backing off. Paul stares at me through a silence nearly as deep as the one following the molding management uproar. Six men and a woman used to endless noisemaking can be strangely silent. And then Paul nods, turning toward the spar shed, with not one urgent word for the rest of the crew.

Wandelaar owner's bath with the "two-unit mouse house," apprentice caught in the act.

With the latches under the case "roof" fussed into place, I'm assigned to haul cradle reinforcement beams from truck to shed. I come back to find Earl has eased the latches inside the finger-holes. He explains how and why, and my puzzlement grows, until I realize he is using the voice he uses while talking with Stanley.

Stainless doesn't wear much, and in any wet weather my doors would jam themselves shut as the wood swelled. His easing left enough play so the catches could not jam. But this time he is talking with—not at.

A couple of days later, with Becky's brushwork done, I set the piece under the mirror, unsupervised. That Friday, the owner is back. In late afternoon, Becky catches me again near her paint shop. Paul has spent at least five minutes impressing the owner with the complication of fitting that particular piece so it would not interfere with his manual sink pump and faucets, she says, and another ten minutes of boat inspection drumming the man's ear with the remarkably fine workmanship the crew has daily poured into the hull. The owner, usually grave-faced, was smiling all the way, she says, and could I show her how to sharpen her scrapers and knife? It's impossible not to like Becky.

The following Monday, I bolt in life-rail stanchions. Below me, Billy threads fathoms of air hose across the trash-heaped shed floor, while Becky with young Tom from the machine shop finishes sanding out the starboard topsides (the hull between deck toe rail and the waterline). Bill and Steve divide their day between wire work and the spar shed. The big lathes now run steadily, a hum you feel rather than hear through the common wall with the machine shop, as they turn out sheaves and winch base plates. A dry dust odor of epoxy begins to drift across from the spar shed, where eighty-five feet of aluminum mainmast is being faired smooth. Paul uniformly applies a drier grit, and the air is full of salt, dust and launch.

17

Doghouse Redux: Stanley

Jug was a young man with magnificent outsize ears, whose proper name I somehow never learned. Jug worked for Paul until his fall term of school began. Given the jobs he got in the yard—a great deal of cleanup—school must have seemed a vacation.

Satisfied that microballoons could do no more to smooth the shape of the hull, Billy set Jug and Becky to fine sanding parts of the starboard side of the hull. Billy explained that microballoons are a sort of chemically agreeable commercial silt that in combination with epoxy made the "mud" he used to smooth any slightly uneven plating on the hull.

While the youngsters made vast amounts of ruddy gray dust, Billy hauled loop after loop of air hose into the big shed, rearranged staging, put on what must have been a life-preserving mask, opened a can or two, and began to spray behind his sanders.

The *Wandelaar* dissolved in my tears, as the shed filled with the most penetrating acrid stink I ever inhaled. If you take the aroma from a swine pen on a steaming hot Iowa afternoon and combine it with tear gas and fine sand, you have the formula.

Stanley and I were setting doghouse window framing, but in moments could barely see our hands, let alone anything else. Earl sprang into action, this time outdoing himself in speed and precision. Shed doors flew open, fans appeared as if dropped from the ceiling, and gradually the choking, gagging and coughing slowed as we all concentrated on just breathing. Particle masks helped, but not much. And only Billy had a mask that really cleaned the air he breathed.

For Stanley and myself, life continued possible because Billy's spray fell rather than rose, and we spent as much time in church with the bandsaw as we did on the hull. Above him, working in and out of the doghouse we managed to keep on with the frame sections.

At noon, I asked Billy what the deadly stuff was. "Hawg Rip," he said in a tired voice, stripping off his Martian mask, "it gives the prime coat a better grip on the hull. Sort of etches it."

And everything else, I thought. It was two more days before I knew that I'd heard wrong, and the real name of the acid was Awlgrip. More than Awlgrip complicated Stanley's and my own joinery on the doghouse windows. The inside framing, done by Jonathan, Stanley said, was installed with a wind ("wynd") in the fairing wood. Plate glass, remember, has to go in flat, and these were relatively huge pieces, a pair on each side, the single sheets roughly fourteen by forty-eight inches. None of the plate had yet been cut, it turned out, and my attempt to straighten out the twisted arrangement by patterning and cutting out a clean flat section of ply produced mostly indignation from Paul, "A waste of wood." But he smiled briefly when, two days after, he found my portside glass was intact. So did I. The smile was rare enough so that when it appeared, life was possible for a day or more.

I was told a story about Jonathan, who left soon after I became an apprentice.

I heard the yarn from two witnesses and in time worked enough beside Stanley to be pretty sure it was not invented. Jon, still in college, was tall, lank and uncommonly hectic in motion. The crew liked Jon, but it seems there was occasional comment on his habit of bounding wherever he went in the shop or on board any boat. There was audible excitement broadcast in Jonathan's every trip from church to hull and back again, and no one had to look to see who was on the rickety bridge between hull and shop; the noise made your head hurt.

On the day Stanley fitted the companion hatch to the doghouse on *Wandelaar*, he asked Steve to help him settle the big lid on its tracks atop the house. While this was going on, Jonathan leaped with increasing energy up and down the companion ladder on his missions between church and doghouse interior fitting. Stanley sighed deeply but said nothing, even when Jonathan's passage twice forced him up from his knees.

Satisfied with the fit of the guide rails on each side, Stanley stood— as a rising thunder inside the boat announced Jonathan's further passage. At bound three, Jonathan came to the foot of the ladder, focused of course on its second step to launch him upward. With care, Stanley drew the hatch lid smoothly shut as Jonathan's foot struck the ladder. There was a solid thud, followed by a clatter of tools and a body tumbling onto the cabin sole. Still looking at Steve, Stanley smoothly returned the hatch to its open position and marched off the boat to the joiner shop, never looking back.

By the time Steve got his breath and a look down the companion hatch, Jonathan was sitting up, one hand testing the top of his head. In his remaining time at the yard, Jonathan moved from here to there and back again with far less thunder and a good bit less speed, and anyone working near Stanley felt only his usual aura of benign intelligence.

18

Launching *Wandelaar*

Many yachts have a number, sometimes engraved or cast in a bronze plate, sometimes cut into the forward transverse timber of a hatch. Her Lloyd's number, Paul said, after hunting me down and handing me a quarter-inch, number nine gouge. He produced a template, reading "No. 597349 NET 58."

"I want you to cut her number here," Paul said, fitting the template between hatch carlins (fore-and-aft timbers on the hatchway sides) and tacking it in place. The number ran to within a half-inch of the hatch sides, leaving little room to maneuver the gouge through the devious grain of the fore timber. I got a lamp, outlined the number, stuffed head and shoulders up into the hatchway, and set gouge against wood. Wrong. The tool only creased the butternut.

I found Paul in the machine shop. For once he was not upset with the time I'd spent searching, "In my chest," he said, "just left—under Stanley's bench."

Earl appeared as soon as I was elbow-deep in the chest, "John! Y'don't rummage round another man's tools, EVUH!"

"He said I'd find a slip here," I said, holding up the gouge. A slip has a rounded shape conforming to the inside curve of a gouge blade. It is possible to sharpen a gouge without a slip, but not simple. And Earl was not pleased to learn the gouge Paul had just borrowed from him needed honing. An apprentice should be older, more forgiving, when he learns his master keeps even one edge less than perfect.

Alone once more in the fore hatch, I had peace the rest of that morning. By early afternoon, I'd evened out my mistakes but was not able to hide one run-out off the final 8. When I found him, Paul came,

Wandelaar, masted, at Paul's float, October 1978.

glanced, said "That looks good," and I was able to breathe again. Earl then had a small round mirror to go in the forepeak, and a half-hour with the vacuum in the forward cabins ended the day. I cannot remember what any one else did in the sheds that day, although I ate my noon sandwich with the rest.

* * *

With her hull painted a gleaming white over a blue waterline and red bottom, she at last officially received her name, *Wandelaar*. Her homeport would be Wickenburg, a town not far from the Vulture Mountains, about sixty miles northwest of Phoenix, Arizona, far out in a high, dry country known as the Sonora Desert. I never learned why.

Assigned to clear debris from staging between the stern and the shed wall, Billy and I found one morning a buxom, smiling young woman who made quick work, without flourishes, of name and port. She told us it was Swedish for "wanderer." When she was done, the bright new name looked somehow small and alone on the forward-sloping flat of the stern. With more debris cleared and some of her staging down, *Wandelaar* still filled up her building shed, the largest at Paul's yard.

A mobile three-sided structure with roof—attached for the past eighteen months to the bay side of the big shed—had to be swung away from the back wall before the yacht could be towed out.

In tours of the sheds and yard, I'd never found a big tractor, and the only truck set with wheels for launching stood on the railway, about a hundred yards from the gilt letters on *Wandelaar*'s stern. A broad, concrete apron ran between the row of building sheds and the seawall/tide line, but nothing resembling a truck or carriage big enough to carry this yacht stood anywhere in sight. By this time I had no doubt that Paul or Earl or both had conjured a levitation system that would waft cradle and hull, swiftly and simply, onto the launch truck at the other end of the shed row, down-slope from the huge winch behind the shed wall.

My illusion was swept away next morning. With several hills of industrial trash removed from the boat's cradle, from the shed west wall, from the corner wheels of the mobile shed, and from the oldest operating war surplus jeep I'd ever seen, John Luke climbed into the jeep, fired it up and backed it into line with the chain and cable we attached to a corner wheel on the shed. With the cable run from building corner to a sheave block hung to an ancient crowbar at water's edge, back to a sheave at the building, back to the crowbar and then to the jeep winch, John engaged the winch and then the clutch. With the slack taken up, the cable broke. John moved the jeep to meet the shorter cable and then climbed out, smiling, and motioned me into the driver's seat. He reattached the cable and signaled me to start cranking. Watching the cable, I noticed that it was dull with rust and dirt, with frayed wire-ends sticking out here and there. Also, that the jeep's remaining canvas top leaked a good deal of light from a number of tears in its fabric, all of which seemed to have a common center above the winch on the back bumper. The mobile shed began to move. Gaining confidence, I gunned the engine. The cable snapped, whipping a new gash in the canvas. I got well down in the driver's seat, to John's further amusement.

"Keep y' head down, naow," he drawled, reattaching the cable. This time it held, and by moving the jeep and the bar a few times, we at last opened the lid, sideways, of the big box confining *Wandelaar*. In daylight, the name on her stern looked more confident.

While this was going on, the last of the staging around *Wandelaar* was dismantled; Paul, Steve, Billy, three men hired for the occasion and occasional others joined to clear dunnage and trash from around the hull and cradle. Under Paul's direction, the gang jacked the cradle and laid rail—plain railroad rail—under each side, pointing toward the shore. With small cast-iron wheels fitted, the cradle was let down on the rails, the cable attached, the jeep winch engaged, and *Wandelaar* rolled haltingly, slowly, quietly toward the North Atlantic Ocean. Then things got less quiet.

Most of the following three days dissolves into those memory snapshots that we wish were real. I don't remember seeing a camera out there on the yard shore at any time while we were moving *Wandelaar* unsteadily north—sideways, of course—to her first bath in the Gulf of Maine; there was just too much going on, and I still have only fragments of it, all with sixty-five feet of cruising ketch looming overhead, ladder attached, lurching down a hasty railroad, towed by a geriatric jeep, lubricated with the sweat of sometimes eight or even ten men, jacking, blocking, shimming rail, a hectic anthill cradling a huge white egg oddly detached from what went on around and beneath.

For three days Paul circled the lot of us, directing, encouraging, stopping us if we tried to rush something out of sequence. Earl and several others worked on board the whole time, jumping to the side more than once, when yet another iron wheel dropped a flange, hull and cradle dropping a foot one time, when a misaligned rail slid out from the pressure on it. Leaving the boat with greater speed than usual, Earl frowned at the jacks being reset, shook his head and vanished inside the shop. He was out again in minutes, to hand us a long wooden rod, "Here, use this t'gauge b'tween the rails," and shot up the ladder once more. At one point *Wandelaar* rumbled firmly retrograde two feet on her own, when the cable parted—which it always did without notice—after its first good stretch.

With the cradle at last lined up alongside the marine railway truck and a loaded pickup chained to it as a brake, the jeep took the slack out of the cable once more, and in one fine smooth twenty-foot glide, *Wandelaar* at last stood on her launch truck, Frank and Paul shouting together to shut down the jeep winch. I think that was the only time I heard Paul's voice raised all that week, an odd thought when the boat had dropped twice, the cable parted like a pistol shot four times, narrowly missing myself and others, and the crew, numbering nearly a dozen at crisis moments, were flat with exhaustion.

Despite this, we began at once to haul oak blocking under her stern, while jacking to bring her plumb when she met the water next day. I think Frank Luke saved my life that afternoon. With Thomas Patrick, Billy and others, I was lugging oak timbers to the cribbing Paul was laying up, aft on the truck. Stepping across from concrete to truck, the timber I carried tapped the cradle. About to drop backward six feet with the oak on top, I found a hand rammed into my belt, shoving me forward to balance once more, Frank's voice calmly noticing, "Give me a little foot room next time, will you?" as his father steered the timber across his stack. Which bulged and blew out five minutes later, hurling eighty- and hundred-pound blocks past Paul and twenty feet down the ways. *Wandelaar* and cradle came down with a thud, popping more heads over the ship's rail, Earl's voice anxious for once, "All right down theah?"

Paul sighed, adjusted his cap, "Ayeh," and bent to his jack once more. I climbed down with Thomas Patrick and started humping block up out of the railway, shaking my head. One of those timbers grazed Paul's shirt on its way out, and he never even blinked. When the four o'clock whistle blew, *Wandelaar* was level, and all of us too wasted to mutter goodnight as we stumbled to our cars.

During the turmoil of moving her to the ways, I learned later, Steve stopped to wipe his face and ask John Luke, I think, why Paul moved his boats this way. John grinned and murmured, "Oh . . . we always move 'em this way."

Most of the time it took to move her, I was too tired to ask anybody anything and only much later realized that, except for the jeep, we could as well have been Greek helots inching argosies down the shore with staves and rollers, rope and wedges. Paul had brought home the best equipment available to form keel, ribs, plate and spars in aluminum. He lived and worked in the age of hydraulic pumps and giant mobile diesel cranes. Nonetheless, every time we did physical labor, he joined in some or all of it and had never to the crew's knowledge rented a mobile crane or a launch trailer. We could have been building something else earning him more money. He liked the process, I finally thought—bruising and wearing, sweat and chaos, Archimedes and brawn—he liked the process that gave muscle and mother wit the strength to move great weights. Something in the force and folly of it moved him. As with all crews, the quick opinion held Paul cheap, hating to part with the cost of crane rental. I still believe the truth is something else. Paul was ready enough to spend for what he wanted, much like the rest of the known world. And in this case what he wanted was his mind and his crew outwitting friction, mass, and gravity itself.

Wandelaar went down the rails next day at high tide, without incident and with Paul at the winch, to loud applause, and rode neatly on her lines. Her designers, McCurdy and Rhodes, were there and pleased and later attended a party Paul hosted for all who helped with the boat.

Having had nothing to do with the shape of her hull and only a little more with the shape of her innards and in spite of her needing spars, rigging, and more weeks of work, I promptly came down with a bad case of postpartum depression. This was not improved by three different men telling me I could make more money up the road at Goudy and Stevens, who were setting up at that very moment for a hundred-foot wooden vessel and wanted joiners.

None of them left Paul, either. I don't want to try to explain this just now. If logic says you go where you can earn the most, we were all nuts. I was utterly convinced that Paul and Earl and Stanley would somehow teach me all I needed to know about the building of boats and that no one else could or would teach me as well. Of course I was nuts. The Owl and the Pussycat or maybe Alice and her looking-glass had charge of my head, or maybe the damned cable hit it once when I wasn't paying attention. If boats demanded reason, there'd be less yachts.

With that noon high tide on a summer-warm October day, she startled us all, gliding off calm and gently as one hopes a new hull will move. Bill-the-Wire said later he was sure she'd snap a cable, so he had a death grip on her wheel as the winch ran out. But she swam free, rocking slightly as she came off the launch sled, easily clearing the dock pilings. Her diesel auxiliary caught, as Bill thumbed the starter. The growing crowd—a good lunch always produces a crowd—clapped and cheered, and John Luke circling offshore in the lobster boat ("She'll stick if I don't—") did a figure eight by way of celebration, escorting her to the dock float. Ashore, he made his way to the tubs of iced beer.

Depleting a can, he inspected his father and the crowd, growing now as food and drink appeared from Verna Luke's, Paul's wife's, kitchen and the coolers in the shade of the sheds. My employer was easing his way along, filling glasses, smiling, needling the photographer, an older gent toting an elderly, well-used Speed Graphic in this day of 35 mm urgency. He had pictured Paul's launch-day trials and triumphs for years. The boss I was beginning to know was a serial—sometimes comic—explosion of impatient energy, while the host I could see this afternoon was a master of social salt and pepper, delighting his guests.

I turned and found John Luke tickled at something in my face. "Son of a gun," he grinned, "ready, wasn't she." He waved a beer at me, "Godamighty, don't look so sober." Something about the middle-aged apprentice amused Paul's son. It may have been a thing less obvious, but two of me would barely make one of John Luke, and the result still couldn't weld a neat seam. Strong, yes, but not neat, and even with John's casual coaching we both doubted I would ever use the grinder less than the torch. He smiled around a third can, "Don't worry, you get t' play with her some more 'fore she goes."

She . . . an ancient Celt in his coracle would have paddled round and round her samurai bow, so alien to all he knew of vessels and saltwater. Joseph Conrad's Captain McWhirr, wise old master of steam vessels, typhoons, and first officers, would have studied her in depth from the corner of his eye not applied to turning cargo into cash and Mr. Jukes into a useful merchant master. *Wandelaar* would have made McWhirr smile. Yachts make many of us smile, but Captain McWhirr's years of studying vessels—sail, wood, steam, iron—and their ways in the sea would comprehend the tensions and strength in her light structure, her sail area, her motion under way.

Against the "more-than-a-year" of others in the yard—and a few for much of their lives had built boats—I had set out in August to help make her accommodation livable, and by this October day it was. But my ignorance of boatbuilding, of hands-on boat work, creating the beautiful shell of a hull, was still complete. *Wandelaar* was in Linekin Bay, carrying some trim and ornament of mine, but all my boatbuilding remained in my reading and my head. I'd come to learn but felt I was not learning enough, especially the art of lofting (the drawing of full-scale lines of every part of the vessel's hull) and the equal art of transferring those lines to wood or metal were still to come. Scribing and spiling had given me a glimpse, but not at the scale of a full hull.

Only long after did I finally see what Paul and the rest had managed to plant in my head and my fingers in ten weeks. One reason I supposed my ignorance was deepening had been out of sight since the sled rumbled down the ways. Earl, thirty years building boats in this yard, came out of the shed into the sharp October sun, looking entirely unlike my lead foreman. The glinting eyeglasses somehow were not in focus; the quickstep feet were slow, the fiercely busy hands idle. I could see a small smile on the tight clean-shaven face, uncomfortable as a new stiff shirt. When Steve lifted a camera to take Earl's picture alongside Stanley, Earl protested, only giving in when Steve reminded him this was his biggest to date.

What Earl knew and Steve and I would come to know was something else again: she wasn't his anymore. This latest spaceship, child of coracle and Canaveral, belonged to somebody else. In one sense, all of us owned her while building; we had pieces of her engraved in our heads and hands, and she had infinite pieces of us, sweat and flesh and blood. And as John Luke said, she wanted lots more work before she could go, innards and rigging, winches and wire, canvas, paint, varnish, and the million layings-on of hands that in the end decide whether such a creature will swim or sink, will change hands or go to the salvage yard or be cherished in one family lifelong, as some are.

The vessel doesn't have to be a yacht, or grand. Look around most any port, and you find trawlers kept like fine yachts and the unhappy opposite: peeling schooners, shabby launches, scarred sorry dinghies. We fall in love with some of them. Earl, while my Barbara and I stayed at the party, looked like a major piece of himself had been cut out and moored at the dock float, where she now was getting serial visitations and petted like the brand-new bride she was, sleek and polished and impatient for Ocean, this alien element we first learned to build serious vessels for, scared as the little puddle of poteen in the skin-and-willow coracle and curragh, awed as Michael Collins off the bung end of the moon. The fact of her in the water put a hollow in my gut, and the beer was not improving it—there were other hollows in sight, and the warmth of families and friends and respite from work wasn't doing much for them, either.

Passing sandwiches, Verna Luke smiled, murmuring that the crew was welcome as any guest to the Scotch. "Maybe more so," she said with a quiet smile and not as an afterthought. All two fingers from the bottle did was persuade me to make my manners and go home, wondering again how I'd got here; if I should stay, when I seemed slow to learn, compared to any of the others. And so tired. It wasn't age, not when men from eighteen to "don't ask" were doing the same thing at my shoulder. Spinning my wheels, maybe, although I was learning a kind of shape-changing cabinetwork inside her hull and was fascinated all day every day by the differences I could begin to see between building and reading about building. All this got mix-mastered with Paul and Earl, John and Frank, Billy and Bill, Steve and Tony, each here for personal reasons plus a paycheck, each sharply different from the others *except* in every case each wanted to make a boat as perfect as he knew how and to learn what each did *not* know, so he could do this better.

In a rare moment of calm and alone with Earl in the joiner shop, I had worked up courage once to ask him if he had worked through some kind of apprentice program or had worked with someone or with a series of builders to learn his skills. His eyebrows lifted briefly, but after a moment he said, "No, I came to work for Paul, and we got along, and I never left. Been here the whole time, thirty years now." And he turned back to his bench, a short history of a lifetime study.

If I wanted to learn badly enough, it would begin all over again tomorrow at seven o'clock. I set my glass down, saw Mrs. Luke long enough to say thank you, found Barbara waiting patiently, and went home. We went out to dinner, and I nearly fell asleep in my salad.

* * *

An apprentice is a compound fracture. You break him of all his old bad habits and break him in to all your own bad habits. If neither of you breaks under the strain, you may have a workman. The moment he's worth his keep, he thinks you've taken him for granted and leaves you for some notional reason like hot coffee or a higher wage or a findable first-aid box. Better make that "multiple-compound fracture." This is not dignified or scholarly, but I still think it's a journal.

* * *

A typical Apterygota is primitive, six-legged and wingless. Encyclopedia Britannica is dead sure of this, immediately after it gives a fine, compact history of "Apprenticeship and Employee Training." Under Earl's relentless eye, it's a great relief to know that someone distinguishes with care between an apprentice and a primitive subclass of insect. And in a job where the principal work benefit was a place on the crew at seven o'clock the next morning, one or two other distinctions began to surface in my October head: If what I'd heard was true, younger men with more boatbuilding in them had applied and been turned away since August, plus one who was hired and soon let go.

In a philosopher you have an apprentice. In the Far East, the very best apprentices often are viewed as Zen masters, which is refreshing to think about, while Earl is glaring at my latest mistake. I had a lot of refreshment in my first few weeks.

19

The State of Mind—

In *Zen and the Art of Motorcycle Maintenance*, Robert Pirsig writes,

An untrained observer will see only physical labor and often get the idea that physical labor is mainly what the mechanic does. Actually physical labor is the smallest and easiest part of what the mechanic does. By far the greatest part of his work is careful observation and precise thinking. That is why mechanics seem so taciturn and withdrawn when performing tests. They don't like it when you talk to them because they are concentrating on mental images, hierarchies, and not really looking at you or the physical motorcycle at all. They are using the experiment as part of the program to expand their hierarchy of knowledge of the faulty motorcycle and compare it to the correct hierarchy in their mind. They are looking at underlying form.

A few minutes early and a few days before her launching, I hike out through the big shed, my steps scuffing tiny echoes down from the drab walls and high cobweb ceiling. With the hull outside, the entire year devoted to what I first saw over Paul's shoulder suddenly gave itself to me: piles of staging, one tower yet to be broken down; torn, discarded, paint-slapped, salt-bitter coveralls; endless winding snakes of air hose and power cable catch my boots; a vagrant mousey, powder-metal smell rides the sea-salt morning air; paint cans lock themselves to concrete with spillage; corners hold jumbled heaps of wood and metal scrap. I pass two smelters, a lead-liquid, dead-cold smell rising from their burnt sides; a scatter of ruined, heavy leather gauntlets, crouching mouse-pockets of constructive wreckage; occasional rusting, bent C-clamps, steel proof of heavy metal and wood willed into place, evidence of fleeting anger and hot haste. One broken C-clamp, the screw literally twisted apart in frustration.

One mummified lunch, walked carefully around for seeming months, a cast-iron salad sandwich and a shriveled plastic apple, neither bitten nor mouse-chewed—what man so furious he hurled his lunch away after five hard morning hours? Do we leave such anger in what we touch that neither bug nor beast will have it?

Furlongs of loose heaving-tackle, surreal arcs of half-used aluminum plate muraling an unlikely screen wall in pale mercury; Heliarc generators, hulking, sullen, rejected, forgotten after months of perfect droning devotion. I stop, and stand, and look. Around the bandsaw, foot-high drifts of silver sand, showered from half a million feet of patient lines traced under impatient eyes anticipating the next bend, organizing cuts so the piece won't land on the wrong side of the bandsaw blade and make more work, more screeching, grinding, howling, droning work than is absolutely needed to make her right.

The motes of dust riding the air high under the skylights run down two sun paths into the plywood and paper leavings of the mold loft and pull my eye to the big outer door. Beyond the paleness inside and the stale hollows and the dark, the sunlit hull lifts solid beyond the framing door, strong and graceful and lifting, no longer the vague, menacing hugeness she was yesterday—not even the same boat. The brilliant wash of sunshine, her first full daylight, dismisses her exhausted womb and troublesome birthing debris.

A little dazzled by the muck and light, I see her separate for the first time, a unity, and maybe when rigged, a beauty. Her lines hold strength and speed. I start toward the big door again, and stop. Earl for once is not doing anything visibly complicated or efficient.

For the first time since I came here, I find him standing quiet, alone in the morning shadow of the shed wall, just standing off and looking at her, silent and utterly still, his hands empty of tools. He has not heard me behind him in the shed. I turn and go, I hope unheard, back to the wire shop to wait for the seven o'clock whistle.

20

The Pulpit and the Pits

The launch party went on, of course, after Barbara and I left, finally dwindling as it scattered to local watering holes, apartments and private homes. The town ambulance went screaming out near two a.m., but their accident was none of ours.

All hands were bright-eyed next morning, in high spirits, when Paul appeared, looking prosperous—a launch is better than a hull in the water; it's money in the builder's bank—bearing a fistful of paper.

Organization had set in again. There was a slip for each of us. Mine read:

- Fix catch in fwd head.
- Fix door catch in stbd shower.
- Hang tiller in lazarette.
- Stowage in lazarette.
- Complete bow pulpit.
- Install boom gallows & pin.

It was written in a strong, round, Palmer Method hand, right out of a wood-fired, shake-roof, spinster-taught crossroads schoolhouse. I had to grin. Whatever his world had done to this man, there was a powerful core of boy in him yet.

The door catches, the tiller and the stowage brought me finally to the pulpit. Somewhere in here I've mentioned mirror clips, stainless steel mirror clips. Compared with the pulpit, they were trifles. Since my escape from the machine shop, I had done no metal fabrication.

A bow pulpit is a spider, mostly legs and on its back, meant to

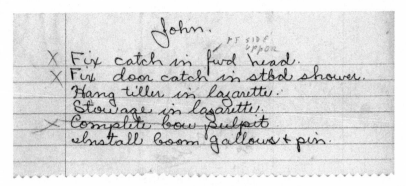

One of Paul's lists.

keep crew from getting washed off the boat while working headsails. Cruising or racing, nobody wants crew in the water except by intent, afterwards, celebrating. I found right away that my skill with files and filing was almost entirely lacking. Frank Luke noticed, and aided by Bill-the-Wire (who installed lighting wire in the tubing, while I wore away welding lumps left at several joints), I got better and faster at creating smooth corners, in between feeding bolts and more wire to Bill, now inside the forepeak.

"Ever do any boat wiring?" he asked.

"No, here's your green," I said.

"What? No, the darker one. John, are you color-blind?"

"Yeah, red-green."

"Oh, shit," muttered Bill, just audible through the fore hatch, "did Steve tell you I'm leaving?"

"No, where're you going?"

"As far 's the Cape with the boat, then come back and renew some of my licenses, electrical, oil furnace, and so on. And my class B drivers. Then go offshore fishin' a while."

"In winter?" I knew the deep-sea boats went out in winter but never had met anyone who actually crewed one—or wanted to. "You been out before?"

"Been out on a friend's boat. It's cold, but you dress for it. And the pay's good if you make a decent catch."

"I think I'd rather be ashore in a Maine winter."

"Me, too, if I could make some money. Promise me you won't do any wire for Paul, hear?"

"Not a chance. Unless he wants Channel 5 on his depth finder."

Wandelaar, mizzen mast, halyards, windlasses; wheel and compass binnacle lower right.

Bill snorted, but Paul did ask, later, and I had to explain why I could match wood, but not his fistfuls of rainbow wire.

* * *

The sixty-five-foot boat at the end of Paul's dock float needed an eighty-four-foot mainmast, a shorter mizzen mast, spreaders and booms for both, plus rigging, winches, sheaves, and a dazzling amount of small stuff to hold all these in place. We manhandled all this over the dock to water's edge, where Mason's derrick barge gently lifted both sticks into place.

Billy hinted that you could find the King's broad arrow up one of Mason's boom timbers and that Mason had repelled his son's up-to-date waterproofing efforts by parking his pride and joy under a local pogy plant drain. Judging by the rich aroma, Billy spoke truth. But Mason and his big, rough barge and boom put both sticks smoothly in place with no paint lost, and a minimum of shouting.

The hard part of all this final fitting out was mileage. Shop to float to shed to float, machine shop to float and back again for pins, storage to float, wire shop to float, again and again. When Frank caught me leaving that afternoon and asked if I would come Saturday to help set some mizzen winches, how could I resist?

The extra cash helped, a little. Remember this was 1978, when blue collar work in Maine had suddenly become my concern; I was happy just to be working at a job that didn't put me in a factory and kept both hands and mind busy.

This didn't stem my worry over the economics of it. Paul started

me, for good reason, at minimum wage. By October the only sign that
I was earning my way was one small raise, which brought my take-
home pay to a tad over $500 a month.

Our first month in Boothbay cost us over $800, and September,
when the car ate its transmission, cost $1150. I was learning good stuff
every day, but I could see our small savings shrink while worry grew
on Barbara's face. My mother was pleased that her son liked building
custom yachts, but when would this begin to pay off? Nervous as she
was, she held her peace most of the time and seemed happy to have us
on weekend visits. I was learning something I had dreamed about all
my life and knew I was getting better at it.

None of which offered a rationale for ignoring better pay up the
road when Goudy's was setting up for the hundred-footer in wood.
Faith or insanity, something said I had to stay the winter in Paul's yard,
or I would lose what I came for. And this was more absorbing, since
I'd had no prior hint of what somehow stirred me the instant I first
stepped through Paul's joiner-shop door. I was surviving, doing joinery,
and could not remember being so happy with work or workplace
before in my life. And if I would stay, then Earl and Stanley would
show me how to build a boat.

With her owners aboard, *Wandelaar* sailed for Greenwich,
Connecticut, at 14:00 hours, Thursday, 5 October 1978. Lyn Smith,
Bill-the-Wire, and Frank Luke sailed with her to finish up mechanical,
electronic, and rigging details, planning to leave her at Cape Cod and
drive home.

By way of celebration, on the Wednesday before, Paul and Mrs.
Luke invited the owners, several friends, and the yard crew and their
families to Paul's "camp" (his word) for evening cocktails. The camp
turned out to be a very private and perfectly beautiful three-room
palace with an in-ground swimming pool across the patio.

Solid drinks and huge platters of hors d'oeuvres induced
circulation well before Barbara and I arrived. Collared almost at once
by one of *Wandelaar*'s designers, Mr. Rhodes, I got a quick review of
recent developments in spar design. Mr. Rhodes turned out to be
the very model of an understanding architect, once I'd explained my
limited acquaintance with his subject. We soon worked out an amiable
student-teacher relationship on the subject of Delrin shims for the
multiple sheaves hidden in jiffy-reefing booms. Then moved smartly
on to Tinsley Island and the parties he had attended as guest of the

St. Francis Yacht Club, on the San Joaquin Delta. My own experience there had been more restful, but the St. Francis, it seemed, from time to time produced parties of style and imagination. I should mention I use "Mr." here, because I never got his first name, and my head was swimming from Paul's fine Scotch.

Paul's party had gained strength and duration by the time Barbara and I left, already fast friends with many folks whose names would vanish with the night. We had a fine time, but I managed to keep seven a.m. firmly in mind.

21

The Augean Stable

I managed to keep a list, so this is verbatim:

24 October 1978

Tuesday 07:00: Lobster boat, aft cockpit bulkhead; hatch, cleat and screw home, then replace.

08:00: 32/17 propeller, 3-blade: detach from display stand in old office, disassemble, clean for machining.

09:15: Short stays, a pair, intended for WANDELAAR; curl and wrap for shipment to mfr., who cut the damn things short.

09:45: SEA SWALLOW, forward anodes (zinc); finish grinding, back with alum. plate & grind fair to forward hull.

11:30: Lunch.

12:30: Anodes—the first pair of backing plates, too thick, replaced with 16th" aluminum & finally faired at about 14:30.

14:30: Pilot work: i.e., help Billy & Doug carry inside & re-stack a load (pallet) of butternut delivered this noontime. In line with shop practice, no stickering, just "pilot."

15:00: Lobster boat, aft deck: prepare for davit mounts & rough out fairing blocks to level & true davits.

16:00: Closing whistle.

For three weeks after the big ketch sailed, the only members of the joiner crew not applied to aviation ("pilot here, pilot there—") were Earl and Stanley. They were just as busy, but their results reduced the damage done the joiner shop over eighteen months, restored windows, and stopped leaks in the roof. After a dry summer, the fall rains felt good but not when descending in a stream through the skylight on your neck at the bandsaw, while I cut up discarded frame patterns from year-old work on *Wandelaar*. Doug Henderson energized and reformed our skills in aviation. In spite of his week watching the crew's ant-heap frenzy while maneuvering *Wandelaar* into a state of grace on the launch truck, Doug hired on at the yard. His first work was to help us deal with the not much put away and damn little swept up in the entire time of the boat's building.

On an axis between the two poles of the joiner shop and the big shed, we plowed through one pile after another, most days hip deep and filthy with what Doug insisted was the study of—"Aviation," he drawled in a fine Houston baritone. "We do a lot o' this in Texas, too, y' know; pahlot here, pahlot there—after a while you're jes' flyin' along."

This much good humor on the other end of a ten-foot timber that had just tried to break my knee was too good to resist. And it continued later, even when Paul installed Doug in the machine shop with the big bronze propeller, offering only the casual instruction that he should, "Get this cleaned up and polished, will you?"

Paul then walked off, leaving Doug bemused. Few doctors come equipped with expertise in the finish and smoothing of yacht propellers. John Luke witnessed their exchange and rescued Doug with files, floats, a demonstration, and the smiling advice that Paul "doesn't always say just what he wants."

Having driven from Texas to Paul to learn boatbuilding (on his way to becoming a naval architect), Doug soon filed his way to an understanding of propeller blades, maybe in excess of what he wanted. After a few weeks in the yard, it was hard for the rest of us to resist just letting a new hire find out by himself how casual Paul was about instruction. It was as if there was so much stored away behind those hawk eyes that he assumed it just poured into whoever his next assignment was confusing. John and Frank, with long experience of their father, had little trouble interpreting his wants. The rest of us, including at times even Stanley and Earl, were fair game.

And I admit to feeling better, once I learned that Stanley and Earl could induce anxiety in our maximum leader. The tip-off with Stanley was a kind of dignity damaged by collision, expressed by an occasional deep sigh and vehement application of whatever tool he happened to have in hand. And whether or not we had heard the difference of opinion between Earl and Paul, the result in Earl was a speed of execution beyond the merely mortal, coupled to a reduction in speech that would have left anyone unschooled in boats unable to follow any instruction he gave his joiners. Cryptic did not describe it. But the effect was to make us ask each other for advice, so the net result did little to slow the work in hand.

But I neglect our weeks of aviation. The floor of the big shed was anywhere from ankle deep to knee deep in combinations of smelter, snowdrift scrap aluminum, work gloves reduced to shreds; short plank, stub bracing, and other wood scraps; discarded coveralls gone at knees, elbows, cuffs and beltline; frozen C-clamps (patiently unfrozen by Steve and oiled into submission); the dead lunch; yards and rods of rope, chain, cable, and not least, two sections of I-beam sixteen inches deep, which had to be moved four times before the crud they held down could be cleaned up. If I repeat myself, it is only because it went on a long, long time, and I'd hate for you to miss the full effect on us.

Behind the big shear lay one of the prize assignments. The shear was a hydraulic guillotine about twelve feet long able to slice through stainless steel and aluminum of alarming thickness. Under and behind it lay two years worth of densely packed steel, stainless steel, and aluminum off-cuts, from minute strips to eight- and ten-inches wide, hip deep. Thomas Patrick was amused by my grumbles at having to deal with this, but was less amused after two days of helping unweave it, strip by strip, to sort and add to each careful stack outside the sheds for later collection by a salvage service. Lyn Smith, the shop's best welder, said it was two years worth. I believed him, long before I was done.

Doug and I, after the lobster boat and *Sea Swallow* were hauled and cradled ashore, also hauled the floats, which took most of another day. Then there was the spar shed, now in storage mode, on the (replaced) dock. This took about a week of hectic hammering and trying to not fall into the bay while shingling.

Sea Swallow came into the middle shed. Bill-the-Wire referred to her—in private—as "Sea Gulp." A stocky cruising ketch, I learned she was Paul's first aluminum hull, built, memory says, about 1968. She looks as if her owner loves her as a home afloat, also as if he trusts Paul implicitly, judging by the personal belongings left aboard. She is here for rub strakes to be mounted below the gunwales, for a permanent aluminum-and-glass dodger (an open deckhouse), for a larger auxiliary diesel, a cabin heating system, and more detailing in her main cabin.

The lovely hull of Paul's own sloop,
Tempting (in my imagination; I never learned
her actual name).

Earl marked out the port and starboard layout of her new rub strakes, handed me a large, deafening grinder, pointed out the cotton in the first-aid box, and smiled.

This morning, 25 October, I leveled and set fairing blocks for davits on the lobster boat's afterdeck. Paul came by, hoping out loud that I would forego the blocks and just "set 'em in there, Jawn!" I suggested that the crowned aft deck would point his davits outboard like rabbit ears on a TV and asked if he wanted his dinghy to look that, careless. He sighed, said, "Well, hurry it up," and left.

As I finished up about 8:30, he surprised me by showing up again, and once more his, "That's well, Jawn," put me in princedom for another five minutes. Released from this to the grinder, I spent the remainder of the day making endless noise and clouds of dust along *Sea Swallow's* port side.

Coming in next morning, I found Billy and Doug heaving one of the smelters up the staging alongside *Tempting*, Paul's own boat, in the little shed bay between *Sea Swallow* and the joiner shop. With this fired up, Becky played a hose stream against *Tempting*'s keel, while retired plumbing lead, salvaged chimney leading, ancient gutters, and recovered fishnet weights were melted down and poured off as fixed ballast. While we all wore particle masks, the net effect (no pun intended) throughout both sheds and the joiner shop was fuming clouds of smoke, carrying a thick reek of flaming fish factory and incendiary outhouse.

My grinder dust combined nicely with the oily smoke to coat nearby walls, crew and clothing with an oily grit that perfumed the place for weeks after, on the rare days when it warmed up in sunlight. That night I left my coverall back of the wire-room door and never took it home after that. Replacement took less effort than explaining.

Somewhere in this tumult, Billy and I helped Earl and Tony finish patching those sections of roof still leaking. With roof decks gently sloping across most of the shed row, we had only to lay out sheets of roofing-felt and swab them heavily with asphalt.

In between work on *Sea Swallow* and *Tempting*, we made further repairs, finished cleaning up *Wandelaar*'s birthing shed, replaced the wheeled shed extension, and as deliveries arrived restocked supplies. Supplies included a semitrailer loaded with aluminum plate in sizes up to six-by-sixteen feet, from thin to very thick—an inch or more.

George's boat had come in a few days before, so we trundled his partly framed daysailer to one side of the big shed door. George was a neighbor and friend of Paul, taken off abruptly with an unheralded heart attack. His widow asked Paul to finish the hull in the yard. Paul agreed, so George's boat a few days later became my first welding job.

Aluminum in big chunks is not light, and moving these sheets soon made Tony, Billy, Doug and me think up ways to lighten the load. Each piece had to come across the transverse I-beam base on opposite sides of the wheeled shed, then be angled sidewise to rest leaning against the big-shed cinder-block wall next to the hydraulic shear and the setup grid.

Under the roof, near thirty feet above the concrete floor, a gantry crossed the entire shed just inside the west (water) door, from the north to the south wall. We knew the block and fall of this traveling lift would pick up at least the bare hull of a substantial boat, so we recruited it, leading the lower block clear outside the wheeled shed to a heavy C-clamp fixed to each incoming plate. With clash of chain and screech of plate we began to make real headway, at least until the gantry carriage edged its way to the gap cut weeks ago overhead in its I-beam rail—to clear *Wandelaar*'s deckhouse as she made her exit.

The noise was deafening, but the damage was mostly to our nerves. The sound of big chunks of metal plate thundering down carries well and carries meaning. All four of us leaped away, three outside into the wheeled shed and Tony behind the shear. With three wheels off its rails, the carriage caught the top of a staging tower that had been moved away for *Wandelaar*'s exit, driving the tower against George's boat, where the tower stopped, groaning slightly. The big plate came free of the chain fall without striking man or gear—but hit wall, I-beam, and finally the shed floor with impressive echoes at every collision.

We dusted ourselves off, counted noses, peered carefully about, and found every man from the machine shop lined up on the safe side of the big press, Paul visibly counting the number of standees. "Anyone hurt?" he called. By the grace of God, nobody was. But we had to get that carriage up off the tower, the tower off George's boat, and the I-beam replaced, before we could move another sheet of stock.

Without exactly delegating responsibility, Paul took the others with him and left Tony and myself to experiment with gravity. A big, husky young man in his early twenties, Tony wore a pleasant but serious face all day at work. When I stopped looking up at the gantry carriage and looked at Tony, he was grinning from ear to ear.

"Boy! Some noise, huh?"

My own ears were still ringing. Some noise indeed. I've never enjoyed working off loose ladders, and that day was no exception. It went on for a long time before I had to give up and call Paul in. The carriage was still eighteen inches from settling on the beam, and I could not see a way to reset one tackle without letting go the chain we used to secure the wheels at the far end.

This was a long while after we temporarily chained up the carriage, cabled the leaning scaffold tower so it couldn't collapse while we finished taking it down, reset ladders a dozen or more times to adjust this or clamp that, moved George's boat farther across the shed, and each time secured each ladder as well as we could.

I found Paul back in the machine shop. He looked up, "Did ye get 'er, Jawn?"

"No. We can't figure out how to pick up the loose end without first letting go my only safety chain."

"Well. I'll come." He looked at it from the floor, then from the ladder top, before calling down, "You'll find a light tackle up the east end of *Sea Swallow*'s shed, and there's some short lengths of chain layin' around. Bring them in and come get me," and he went back to his bench, after sending Tony to another assignment.

The chain took some scouting, but I turned up three or four pieces and set them by the ladder with the tackle. Paul was watching the machine-shop door and came as soon as he saw me enter.

It was a relief to find out that even Paul needed time to unravel whatever mistakes I'd made. I sent up chains and tackle on a light line tied to his ladder. He danced the top of his ladder back and forth more than two feet at times, gaining an inch or two in height with each purchase. When I moved to anchor the base of his ladder, he waved me off and said to stay clear but to draw up or slacken the primary tackles as he directed.

That looming weight of gantry iron overhead had made me stop thinking, and he knew it but never said anything about it. In a little more than an hour, the outboard wheels rolled safely onto the I-beam track, and Paul set a C-clamp behind them.

"Bring up th' I-beam section, clamp it in place; then set up one o' th' weldin' generators an' call me."

He returned to the floor, squared his cap and paced off toward the machine shop once more. It took a search to find the missing beam section, but find it we did, and Paul was up the ladder showering welding sparks as the closing whistle blew.

The extension ladder we used was light in weight and looked unreliable to me. I had no time to think about my own safety while up there but a great deal of time to watch Paul while he dealt with it. I had trouble sleeping that night, first with visions of myself falling off that ladder, then of my boss crashing dead on the concrete floor at my feet. Our sparring matches aside, I liked my boss. The echoes in the shed went on a long while in the dark, but I finally slept. The rest of the plate came inside with no trouble at all.

22

George Resounding

"We worked through yesterday so we could have the Friday following Thanksgiving off," I wrote to my father on 19 November 1978. "I'm not persuaded that six days inside a gong being struck is a rational way to earn a living, but it develops one's powers of concentration. The layup of an aluminum hull gives nothing away to your local boiler factory in matters of decibels."

We refer to this hull as both "George" and "Carey," as friends always addressed its owner. George Carey was Paul's good neighbor and friend and was building, in aluminum, this open-cockpit racer/daysailer, intending two bilge keels and what appears to be a daggerboard/centerboard. With most of the frames in place and two plates on the hull, George was taken in the midst of life, doing something that he enjoyed when his heart attack came. I can think of worse ways to go, although it is hard on the near and dear when there's no warning. Paul has agreed to finish and I think to sell the hull for Mrs. Carey.

George is about thirty foot overall, with a hull shaped round as an overgrown dinghy. Lately I came across a photo of a big overturned Irish curragh that with bilge keels hitched on and with a less aggressive bow would look remarkably like George.

Earl was displeased with the fairness of some of George's framing, so he had Tony and myself grind away at several, even before she was set up plumb and level at working height. When grinding didn't do it, we literally cut out framing between ribs until the offending metal could be clamped fair between other ribs that measured according to plan, then we tack-welded new cleating in to hold all in place. As soon as Earl's batten (a long limber lathe used to set down and transfer lines) bent fair across all framing, Tony and I began cutting plate, while Earl and Paul shaped this on the thumper.

Anchored in the floor at the northeast corner of the big shed, the thumper is the biggest vertical hydraulic ram I have seen, at a glance the shape of a monster guillotine. The operator, by controlling the drop, force and shape of the ram head, can hammer big flat plates of aluminum into the bewildering variety of bi-radial curves that make up the hull of a sail- or power-boat, one plate at a time. The sound of the thumper is the deep hum of a big hydraulic pump, punctuated by repeated thumps as the hammer drops. The noise it makes is muted, gentle even, until you notice that each strike shakes the floor.

It is ancient anvil work, minus the smoke, sparks, fume and mystery. The shape and force of the hammer slightly spreads at each drop the metal face under it, gradually shaping an arc in the plate. To reduce or flatten a vexed convexity, you turn the plate over and thump the concave side. The operator, nearly always Paul, can work a small, light piece alone. But a big chunk can take three, even four men to move, with the operator guiding by hand signals, as his thumb repeatedly drops the hammer with a force ranging from delicate through infinite degrees, to earth shaking.

It all works like this. Earl scales a plate off the plan, marks for cuts, which Tony and I saw with screaming circular saws, our ears plugged as well as possible with cotton, our eyes protected with safety goggles from a steady hail of tiny shreds of aluminum. The trick of cutting sweeping curves in a plate is pure and neat—drop the blade just enough to cut clear through the sheet and always cut outside your mark, trimming to bring it fair. As long as the blade is sharp and the teeth properly set, the saw will cut curves in aluminum all day.

As each big plate comes out of the stack, it is swung up onto the forming table, where one of us rough-sands each side before any other work is done on it. Tony and Steve explain that this takes enough oxidation off so that a weld will adhere readily at any point. Then Earl marks and we cut. Stanley makes his peaceful way past us now and then, but mostly keeps a long way between his ears and us.

Once the thumping is done, Earl sets the plate while Tony and I clamp. I am still too new to not be eager, so have asked to try tack-welding. Lyn Smith has been doing this but is getting gray with dragging his gear from *Tempting*'s shed back out to George, then back to *Tempting*, and welcomes even novice help. Earl shrugs. Paul is amused, always anxious to see progress. Paul agrees. For a few days, Lyn and I drag our TIG welding guns, spool and cables through the three occupied boat bays, until Paul hires Ivan Philbrook to do the seaming on George.

In between making Tony jump with contact sparks from my efforts with the welding gun, I pry all the answers I can out of Lyn and Ivan both. My efforts at a neat seam never really get beyond almost neat. At last I have an answer from Lyn: it is penmanship, combined with ears. You need just enough amps to puddle but not melt plate; and the puddle, endless small pools advancing down the seam, needs the wrist of a fine scribe. I walloped both my hands on concrete in a boyhood fall, so my script handwriting has never got beyond barely legible. I can hand print a reasonably clear line, but the puddle needs a smooth roll, minute after minute. I will probably never do better than tack plate, given any amount of practice.

It turns out that I'm a decent cutter, so in between tacking and cursing my sketchy seaming, I take on as much sawing as I can. The thing that makes me a bad welder makes me a good cutter; that stiff wrist holds a clean line with the saw. Back and forth we go, George beginning to look like a hull and *Tempting* almost yacht-like, despite the raw metal, with her pretty, oval cockpit taking shape.

Earl: "John, you might's well shift to t'other side o' th' bo't while Tony's settin' up that bulkhead."

John: "Well, I'd rather be in Tony's way than your way."

Earl (teetering on *Tempting*'s gunwale): "In my way anyway, so what's the difference?"

John: "Hell, I've been there since August. I'd like to get out of it for once!"

Earl: Broad grin and short chuckle followed by thundering retreat to the joiner shop, the equivalent of anybody else's falling down laughter. Earl and I may yet work out how to live with each other.

Letter to my father, 7 December 1978:

> We are, still, in the middle of *Tempting* and got her cabin exterior (i.e., coach-roof) about finished this week. The noise of working big and little bits of aluminum is not describable, it is often not bearable by the merely mortal. I've already lost hearing in the high frequency range, and nothing much seems to salve except for Kleenex stuffed well into the ear canals.

The muffs are literally too bulky, and get knocked off by every projection in the hull. The best plugs just don't fit my screwball outer ear—the right one keeps dropping out like clockwork. So I screw in (another) tuft of Kleenex, which cuts the worst of the decibels generated by saws and grinders. In spite of which, it's often like working inside Big Ben at noon.

But we survive, and laugh more than once a day, so it goes pretty well. I will never develop the feel for aluminum that I have for wood. Wood to me is a live thing even with the tree felled and sawn, and I seem to relate better to live things.

This power of fire in the fist does tall things to the imagination: I begin to see why, for all their working life, some men can do only steel and iron. It is their fire that makes it grow: When clothed, the structure is fixed in skyline memory, theirs always at any glimpse—their fire gives it shape, dimension, force, character. Building is permanent in their life, its center and horizon.

I wonder, staring through my mask at the arc and puddle, Did the inventor of arc welding actually draw a clean bead along a seam? Or did he stand back and watch some nameless mechanic like myself complete his miracle? Probably, I begin to think, he did the latter. Theory is not practice. I can "sweat" (solder) a decent joint in copper plumbing pipe. A journeyman plumber can set up and sweat four or five joints in the time I take to be sure of one. What did the inventor of arc welding feel the first time his hot wire welded itself to the plate? What did he see, in his guts? Because it takes somebody with guts to play with amperes, with electric fire, however small or well aimed. It delights me to see a hull form over these stark ribs. If he saw even half the potential, it must have been heart-stopping to see, at one leap, what his new tool could do. And if he was instead methodical, his step-by-step discoveries must have kept his adrenaline high for weeks.

I try to persuade Paul to send me to tech school, at least long enough so I get a speaking acquaintance with the proper settings for the welding generators and perhaps understand the numbers identifying the plate characteristics. He just shakes his head, "Ahsk Lyn, 'r Ivan, they'll tell ye—"

Well, yes and no. Ivan hired on to finish seaming plate on George and of course shares what he can, so I will tack properly. But he wants the whole finish job, not just part of it. And Paul shows instant concern when two of us were caught in conversation, so I get my knowledge in bits and chips.

Lyn Smith knows I'm not going to replace him or any other metal worker in his lifetime, so I learn a bit more from him, but never enough, I feel, to be sure I'm using the proper amperage on the given thickness of plate or laying in the most useful thickness on the seam.

As soon as I picked up a MIG gun the first time, Bill and Steve assured me I'd never get to touch another stick of wood. This turned out to be almost true, for days at a time, but with the pleasure of feeling like a functioning part of the process, of helping to grow these shining whales in the sheds, the absence of woodwork lost the bitter part of its sting.

When Paul finally wanted me to seam plate, I settled on the habit of hunting him down and making him come inspect at least my first lines of puddling. For a few days he kept his patience, but at last put a stop to this nonsense by sending me to Lyn or vanishing altogether the moment I dropped my helmet and struck an arc.

When Earl will let himself be maneuvered into talking, he says he is bored with the metalwork already. "Dirty, noisy, boring work," he allowed yesterday in a moment between plates. He has done this metal work twelve years now. Watching him, I see no sign of boredom, only of focus on the hull shapes and on what Steve and Billy, Tony and I do to and with them as they grow.

Tony yells at me when I shower him with sparks as the arc strikes. He didn't protect his face with more than a casual glove for several days when we began, and his boyish round face turned a glowing pink from industrial sunburn before he started to use a helmet while setting saddles and wedges. Despite the leather gauntlets and a leather apron provided by the shop, my work shirts are peppered with holes from hot sparks.

"Gas welding, arc welding, and resistance welding," says Britannica. com, "all appeared at the end of the 19th century. The first real attempt to adopt welding processes on a wide scale was made during World War I. By 1916 the oxyacetylene process was well developed, and the welding techniques employed then are still used. The main improvements since then have been in equipment and safety."

Ivan thinks that Paul's rigs, able to weld both steel and aluminum, cost about $5,000 apiece. In between my constantly ringing ears, I'm perfectly absorbed in this November howl of saws and clangor of wedging hammers—in a point of light and the minute volcano it makes on the next tack. Second by second, minute by minute, the boats grow. The middle-aged apprentice-cum-welder making near-minimum wage at a job he just begins to think he understands is oblivious of the fact that he is happy.

23

The Fire that Binds

Today is Friday, 17 November. Tony clamps and braces the last plate on George this morning, while I tack it down fair with its neighbors. He does not grouse when I finish up by once more showering him with sparks. Beyond the gauntlet on his holding hand, his shirtsleeve is a fine sieve up to the elbow.

Ivan will come in over the weekend and finish seaming George's plate; also perhaps fit her bilge keels. I still am not practiced enough to be a finish welder. Looking at George now, I guess the hull she most resembles is a 505 class boat I saw raced off San Francisco, though she has more beam and I think harder bilges and a shallower draft. Not that it will matter to anyone but her future owner. In tacking her plate, I'm certain I left lumps along seams. Some I ground out with the big disc sander, some Ivan re-melted, as he brought his seam along. Earl is satisfied that his batten shows a smooth run anywhere he lays it across the hull. And if Earl is satisfied, then Tony and I have set every edge of every plate fair with its neighbor, and she will measure to specification, should anyone feel the need.

Tempting now sports a wonderful oval cockpit, an auxiliary engine down below, a couple of forward bulkheads, a deck flowing smooth, bow to stern, and a hull deep enough to make her a comfortable cruising boat for a couple. Earl told me Paul's friend Aage Nielsen, who specialized in drawing yachts to cruise under sail, designed her for Paul. My education somehow advanced from clawing my way upward by observation to whole minutes of vocal transmission from Earl, but I had no idea just when I had moved in his mind from aggravation to asset or how long this happy state might last.

At the spar shop welding bench lurks yet another machine, a more complex MIG unit gleaming with knobs and switches that Lyn adjusts with perfect patience, sober calm. When Paul settles in at this bench, his brow furrows, and often by noon his temper harrows, depending on the thickness of metal being welded, multiplied by his incoming phone calls and the number of times we interrupt him in mid seam.

The Lyn Smith Shorthand Approved Welding Workshop turnes out to be one compact sentence, "You mostly play it by ear and eye, John," which is true as far as it goes. Over time and with much practice, I begin to produce fewer blow-holes and wretched lumps and more short lengths of clean, solid seam—when Earl is elsewhere, at first, and after a while with him actually holding plate or working wedges.

To bring down a plate too high, we welded aluminum saddles over the high spots, wedged the plate down to dimension, tack-welded it to ribs, intercostals and adjoining plate and then broke off the saddle. It was a triumph one morning to bridge a quarter-inch gap between very thin plates, using a dot-and-bead trick Lyn had showed me. My first neat row of volcanic puddles along the seam—gray and bland—when I raised my helmet to look was so classically clean and secure that I promptly blew a half-inch hole as soon as I next triggered the gun. Tony just shook his head, "Got cocky, huh?" We shrugged and got on with it.

A cold arc makes ugly lumps and a weak joint, when it joins at all. An arc too hot will blow holes in the work-piece, a mistake that often needs a second workman to hold a backing plate when the finish seamer comes to that joint. This is to be avoided at all costs, because it costs.

Plating a hull, the tacking and seaming are often done while grinders, saws or sanders are working over the welder's head, sometimes two or three at once. No matter how you pack your ears the din is wicked, but that line of puddles has to stay clean, at least clean enough to hold fast when ground level.

Lyn Smith was unfailingly patient and helpful, but seldom got much lodged between my ears before Paul or Earl sent one or both of us in opposite directions. As a result, my efforts at welding for most of that winter were the result of disjointed and partial directives, half-asked questions and pointers delivered in segments, sometimes an hour or more apart. It was a fractured education that gave me little confidence in doing more than beveling edges and building up a bead probably too thick with repeated passes of the gun, which Earl and Steve and

Billy and the known world then had to grind down before work could proceed.

Nonetheless, I welded, working on structure and seaming on parts of five hulls before I was done, and nothing broke or had to be redone once I got it in. By spring I finally knew my problem was not in my wrist but in my head, and at last a little confidence arrived. A little confidence, of course, can be a dangerous thing.

Oh, we are building boats! New pieces are in place at the end of every day; *Tempting* and *Sea Swallow*, are banged and burnt and caressed and ground into variations on the theme of yacht, and Stanley is working out toe rails for *Tempting*, in long, sweeping planks of solid Thai teak, two inches thick. Walking past Stanley's bench the air is dense with teak incense so strong you can almost smell the elephant that towed the log to the river above Rangoon. Heaven smells like this, and God hired Stanley to make these shavings, so it IS!

I am helping build boats. I am a pocket of poverty so deep, thanks to the transmission, that I suppose any minute now I will reach critical mass and vanish into my own cosmic black hole, possibly sucking Earl and the yard in behind me. I am so happy I am oblivious to this and almost everything except the boats and a bath and supper come nightfall.

Sometimes now I can explain part of what I do to Barbara, in words and drawings understandable. This amazes us. Her Iowa childhood did not include yachts, nor much floatable beyond her father's dog swimming the creek. I come home to our apartment at Boothbay Harbor and babble and am understood. I fall asleep writing to my father and am understood. I know not much and am understood. I need to be hit with one of Stanley's glorious planks. Tony thuds up the gangway and sets the last of the deck plate down on *Tempting*, "Zap it right there." And I do.

Done with tacking plate for a while, so Earl shows me where the ducting will run in *Sea Swallow*'s accommodation, under shelving, behind casework, around existing cable, pipe and equipment. He scratches his ear and resettles his tan cap, frowning.

"I think the stuff'll melt," he mutters, referring to the four-foot-long PVC pipe Paul wants used, "but he says t' try it," then shoehorns himself once more under the midship cockpit sole to grind away at the many pieces of boat keeping a new, much larger, auxiliary diesel from settling into its new home.

Because he has to cut away and rearrange structure, Earl will not put Tony or myself into the bowels of the boat. The new engine has lumps in places the earlier one did not, and every rib and intercostal in way of it has to be replaced with equal or stronger structure. Earl doesn't want to try to explain, so has spent hours over the past two weeks, doubled up in the half-dark, grinding away around his feet, fitting one shining stick of aluminum after another to alter space and redirect loads and forces for when she goes back in the water. Getting Lyn or me to tack the new costal in place, he goes to his bench in church to recover for a while or sharpens a tool or lays out work for one or another of us— Billy, Tony or me. Steve has risen to another plane, and his talk over lunch spills enthusiasm all over us: Steve is lofting.

High above the big shed and its repaired gantry, the plywood floor of the mold loft has been repainted a fresh white. Steve has been taken off *Sea Swallow* to help Dick Lagner scale the lines for a new forty-eight-footer, a sloop by Germán Frers (pronounced "Hermann Frayrs"), an Argentine firm of naval architects.

Your home ashore is composed chiefly of straight lines, drawn by your architect or composed by eye and your experience of loads and forces affecting walls, roofs and floors. It is quick work to scale up a straight line on a drawing to its full dimension on a plank. The average sailing yacht has three curving surfaces, two unique ends, mysterious appendages, and no external straight lines at all. The science of hull hydrodynamics is built up carefully and slowly from several thousand years of "try it and see." As in medicine, art is a substantial, material, intrinsic part of the science. How we get from the architect's cautious curves on paper to the gleaming whale in the shed is done slowly—and with care. Steve is now helping with this; he is a kettle boiling with new knowledge.

As nearly as possible, a perfect straight line is drawn down the loft floor. The three dimensions drawn in two dimensions are scaled up to full size, working from station points along this line and perpendicular to it, using a "table of offsets" (numbers in feet, inches, eighths of an inch) that establishes a given point on the hull at a given distance from some point on this centerline.

Lofting is the careful measuring and marking process that scales up the boat's lines and the molded shape of her hull sections to full size. Just why lofting should carry the whiff of alchemy with it, I've never been able to learn. The old boys, including His Britannic Majesty's naval shipyards, often worked with scale models and half-models, drawing lines plans only after they had a hull to measure.

The patron saint of modern writers on boatbuilding, Howard Chapelle, in his *Boatbuilding*, pursues the lofting of a sailing skiff and a Hampden boat for sixty-nine pages. He closes his first paragraph with this caution: "Plenty of time must be allowed for the task and it should be borne in mind that there was never a boat built in which too much lofting had been done."

Judging by Earl's struggle with *Tempting's* transom, which for more than a day resisted all efforts to make it meet the boat's sides and sternpost, some local opinion differed on the value of careful lofting. But Earl made the transom plate fit, and it looks fine. I only wish I had not been detailed to another part of the boat while Earl was muttering his mantras.

The thermal theory in *Sea Swallow* is to use a heat exchanger close to the transom exhaust outlet and lead BTUs through four-inch PVC pipe into her accommodation forward, amidships, and in the owner's cabin aft. Her new engine is almost in place, and this may be reason enough for Earl to look less hectic, considering the effort it cost him to squeeze it into the existing engine room. My piping contribution is on hold, while I await arrival of flex tubing, reducers, and vents for the cabins.

So I am not mistaken for idle furniture, I work on the main cabin bunks and (to allow piping beneath later) raise the owner's cabin bookshelving two inches. Across the two cabins, the change in height and cleating of the various pieces takes a day and a half.

On an errand to the big shed, I vary my day with a visit to Steve and Dick Lagner in the mold loft, high under the roof. All trash has been cleared away except for the few wood scraps near the bandsaw, which will later cut plywood for molds used to establish and mark the shapes of the vessel's ribs, deck, stem, stern, keel, and floors. In a vessel, a "floor" is an athwartship beam joining two sides of a vertical frame, also called a "rib."

Lagner studies the print, mutters a comment to Steve, and on hands and knees measures sections of floor near his straight baseline, laying down pencil dots again and again. Steve picks up a batten, fixes it in place on Lagner's dots and lines, using small sculpted lead weights to hold its edge precisely on each dot, and draws a long, clean curve. Half of one rib now has been lofted from the lines plan to full scale, from keel centerline to sheer line (top edge of the hull). The full rib can be molded from the half by drawing and cutting a mirror image of the half-rib.

The stillness and the stark light of this cave-in-the-ceiling suggest a refectory daily scrubbed for inspection by Brother Prior, possibly God himself. The men wear soft-soled shoes or go in stocking feet to prevent scuffing the pencil lines wiring their way across the white floor. I am enough aware of Lagner's focus to simply stand silent and watch. He glanced up when I reached the head of the stair, but after that did not look at Steve or me.

Move slightly down the line; examine plan; measure; make sequential dots. Steve then sets the batten, double-checking to assure that its edge just touches each dot on the curve, that the curve runs smoothly over its entire length, then draws the single slim line along that edge—again and again. Steve looks up briefly and grins.

I go away, far away to the din, clank and whine aboard *Sea Swallow*. We are, indeed, building boats, using traditional methods and hot-dog technology, some of it hot-dogged in defending ancient Athens. You could make a case that it was really the Piraeus shipyards in 480 BC that won Salamis.

In an age when you rammed the enemy ship with your own vessel whenever you could, the Persian fleet of about 800 galleys found itself lured into the strait between Salamis and the Greek mainland. Themistocles turned his triremes and attacked. With a fleet of about 370 vessels, he sank close to 300 of the Persian fleet while losing only 40 Greek ships. The Persian losses in life and shipping were enormous. Xerxes was forced to retreat. I wonder if Themistocles bought his shipbuilders a drink when he got home. Greece would certainly not, for all its faults, have prevailed without them.

24

Dear Virgil—
from a Letter to Barbara's Mother

18 December 1978

Dear Virgil,
      . . . . .

What do I actually *do*? Well, for the past week I've been installing cleats in *Tempting*. She will be Paul's own new boat, a sloop with auxiliary diesel engine, about 38 feet overall length. Cleats are little square columns of wood, 3/4" x 3/4" of varying length, fixed to hull-frames and bulkheads (internal transverse walls of a vessel) to which the ceiling is later fixed. The ceiling in a boat, I should mention, may well be the wall against which you steady yourself in a seaway; technically, it's the internal wooden skin which, painted or varnished, the owner sees when he's inside his boat. But it has to be solid, hence the cleats. Today, I fitted a couple of bulkheads which, looked at directly from above, went like this: [drawing now missing].

The big teak plywood flats are glued and screwed to the little triangular pieces, and often to each other. The result is a very strong internal bracing structure, as well as a wall to keep the head (bathroom) private. [Virgil in her more than seventy years had never seen a yacht.]

The most entertaining thing about building a yacht (to a joiner, at least) is its continually changing shape. The vessel's only true horizontals and verticals are internal. Every other surface bends, to a greater or lesser degree, as you work along the hull, deckhouse, or cabin side.

The men I work with, like the hulls and materials, are
not average. From what I can learn, Paul has never overpaid
anybody, but the people who come to his shop and stay could
literally work anywhere (I've heard) at far better wages than Paul
pays. Paul's idea, and that of his joiner-foreman, Earl Dodge,
is to give new men a blood bath for the first week or so. If
they don't have what the work requires, they soon leave of their
own accord. For instance, I spent my first week at the shop
on bended knee, doing a lengthy act of contrition to the port
locker in *Wandelaar*'s main cabin. If you have ever tried to work
for hours on end while crouched kneeling on a hard surface,
you have some idea of Paul's weeding-out process.

The . . . problem I had at the beginning was to learn the
conventions; that is, what is the usual, or agreed best way to
create a certain piece of equipment or furniture in a custom
yacht. My bosses vary in their teaching: Paul will tell you one-
half of what you need to know to do a certain job, and then
disappear. By the time you need to know something more
specific, he's changed his mind about how he wants it done,
so you end up learning two (sometimes three) different ways
of doing it. Earl, his joiner-foreman, will work with you for
about half the job, dropping hints in abrupt Yankee as you
work. You have to translate these into Yankee, and sometimes
into English, since they often are delivered while someone is
adjusting aluminum plate overhead.

—With a large hammer and much energy! And Earl never
shouts. He groans a lot, especially at me, but never shouts. Earl
then vanishes, and if later on you can find him he just grins
and says, "I showed you, once!" and goes back to whatever he's
doing. But it works, and I learn.

What even the senior men try to avoid is a set of instructions
from both Earl and Paul. Neither one does anything the same
way. It takes a brave (or desperate) man to sort out one of these
joint sessions and get through with a whole skin. The two men
have worked together for thirty years, so no blood is drawn.

Billy has mastered the process so well that he knows exactly
how and when to leave the two of them in deep discussion
without either noticing he's gone. He says the signal is the
second time Earl pulls on the peak of his cap. But this only

works well if both are talking at once and Paul sounds a little disturbed. Billy has the ear of a choir-master and the instincts of a seasoned Secretary of State.

Doug Henderson despairs of our ever getting some respect for decent pronunciation. About malleable metal woven cable he says, "it's WAUGHR, f'heaven's sakes, not WYAH!!"

It is December and with two raises I am making $4.00 an hour, while going broke due to a California car that should never have crossed the Sierra Nevada in the first place. And I am still happy. Most logics I know of define this condition as delirium. I'll settle for it.

. . . . .

John

25

Balance, I Think—

The rest of the world pursued different obsessions, more or less, while I pursued the structure of a boat. Or maybe the good building that makes a beautiful boat. I managed to ignore much of the outer noise, but the world is older, smarter, and kept its elbow in my ribs. Letters exchanged with my father and others reminded me that life existed beyond Paul's winter dock.

While I helped build boats, Barbara and I hosted a serial Thanksgiving feast for three families and survived a Christmas. We also survived an apartment house furnace venting itself routinely through our living-room floor, aided slightly by a nearby chimney once clear in flue but not now breathing well.

Barbara was still recuperating from two hip replacements. Wives game to follow husbands into strange climes and odd work are uncommonly brave, anytime. A wife

Hull ninety-six (opposite) shortly before slinging to roll upright and (below) while plating. Hull ninety-five (above) starboard forward framing, "strongback" upper right; center line is ground zero for all frame measurement.

willing to follow a husband into near poverty among strangers is rare indeed.

My uncle died. When I was little, my Holt uncles were physically near, kindly but distant men. Charlie Sherman, married to my father's sister, was dear because he knew little kids liked to laugh. However far off, he was never absent in spirit. While my parents were approximately still together in New Bedford, I wandered off to Chancery Street one time, where Frances hugged me and Charlie made me laugh about something. The aunt or uncle who does this will never fade, present or absent, and often they lifted my mother out of that day's sorrow.

The world beyond Boothbay and home was full of panic. Jimmy Carter was president, abused by the media before, during, and after the Tehran Embassy debacle. TV reflected astonishing numbers of Manhattan and Washington, DC homicides; here in Maine, we killed people with cars and winter on a dependable schedule, and I suspect spring came late but cannot remember my evidence for saying so.

I was building boats. Earl now sometimes spoke to me slowly enough so I could comprehend; Stanley sculpted daily and gently at his long bench, past which I tried to wear a furrow in the floor, and at Paul E. Luke, Inc., hulls number ninety-six and ninety-five began to be more than paper and a gleam in an owner's eye.

By early winter IBM was under assault by The United States of America on grounds of running a monopoly, and it seemed to me that the exercise would benefit lawyers to the exclusion of all others. By February I had enough energy left one night to type out five pages explaining all this to my father, plus a thumbnail theory of American voting habits and the reasons I thought Santa Clara County might soon

Hull ninety-five, the bones now mostly in frame, to become sculpture.

Hull ninety-six, plated and rolled upright. Next will
be decking, more internal framing, bulkheads, and
on and on and —

eclipse San Francisco in population and wealth. This may have been
due to inhaling argon gas while welding. By February I had just noticed
that the hull I supposed was number ninety-five was actually number
ninety-six, and we'd just begun framing number ninety-five.

In my finite view through the welding mask window, number
ninety-six was an infinity of intercostals holding ribs in rigid rows
that suggested a seagoing hogshead split along its staves. It seemed
a comfortable cruising hull, but without anything special about it.
Number ninety-five woke me up. Or maybe Paul bought a better
grade of argon to surround my neater welds. More than any other
we built, number ninety-five was the boat I wanted to see through
to her launching. Number ninety-five had presence, panache, power,
charisma, all rolled into one. She also had frames set fifteen and a half
inches apart, mostly by me, at Earl's orders. My shins were still scarred
from staggering through the whale ribs of my new beloved, bleeding
into my boot tops. Saw-cut aluminum has unforgiving edges.

The name Germán Frers rose on my horizon; I learned that this
man or his office designed number ninety-five. She made me want to
be there in the shed at seven a.m. If the ailing car had failed, I would
have walked to work. For no reason I can identify, number ninety-five

became absorbing as soon as a few of her midship frames were settled on the "strongback."

If you think you could never be so afflicted, let me assure you your Hull Number Ninety-Five will find you. Others have been reported to me, in several shapes, guises and characters, including canine and bovine. By nature or personality or vision, we are drawn to different shapes. You cannot escape.

My photos of the two hulls finally suggest a reason for my fascination with number ninety-five. Number ninety-six is, even in the shadows of the shed, a pleasant, round, gentle hull based on soft, flowing forms. Number ninety-five, still in frame, upside down in my flat fluorescent snapshots, has a firm jaw, an attitude, a no-nonsense deep keel, and her maximum breadth is aft of midships, giving her a tuck in her bottom that even Earl found challenging, when we set plate between her keel and rudder skeg.

But I digress: history ignored will repeat itself. At this writing, the Car of the Year is the Plymouth Horizon, according to Motor Trend magazine. It costs $3,787 plus tax and "destination charges." The day I started at Paul's, *The New York Times* reported that Charles Scribner's Sons would, after five generations of family operation, merge with Alfred A. Knopf, Jr.'s Atheneum Books. December 10, 1978, *The Times* advised that a floppy disk was eight inches in diameter, cost $8.00, and carried about three hundred pages of manuscript, writing on your very new computer.

At that writing, I had seen photos of computers but not the real thing. On 15 December, 1978, the Dow Jones Industrial Average stood at 812.54. Microsoft was not visible on most horizons. IBM engineers in 1972 had supposed that a machine able to arrange the contents of 3,000 punch cards would focus a reasonable day's work for an operator.

On New Year's Day 1979, *The Times* noted, "Authorities deny the Shah will leave soon." On 1 February 1979, Khomeini returned to Iran after fourteen years' exile in France. And so on, and so on—I didn't care. The only objects I cared about were inside Paul's sheds, and the only people—those at home and in the sheds.

I had reserves of energy beyond any I'd expected in my forties and began on 16 January 1979 a long and more-than-usually cheerful letter to my father. It repeats a couple of things you've seen, but its building sequence may be the best of any description I wrote him.

Dear Dad,

. . . . .

Hull 96 is to be yet another cruising ketch, with auxiliary diesel power. She has good lines, from what I can see so far. Hull #96 begins with a horse, or strongback. Two steel I-beams are laid parallel on the shop floor, cross-struts are welded between them and, centered on these crossbeams, a row of vertical steel posts is set.

Atop this row goes the principal object, a third steel I-beam which must be straight and true within 1/16" for its forty-foot length. This upper beam is bolted together in ten-foot sections, post-to-post in the most ancient Greek fashion. Great energy is spent in getting this thing straight, because on it are lined up all major frames inside the boat.

The actual hull, sans deck, is done upside down, frames, intercostals and plating, with the frames suspended upside down on and from this steel Stonehenge. It takes the best part of three weeks to loft the lines and get out the frame floor patterns, with two men going full tilt that whole time. Once most of the patterns are cut, framing begins with the cutting and shaping of aluminum extruded bar and T-shaped bar stock for hull and deck frames, and thick sheet-aluminum stock for the floors and keel framing.

"Frame numbering, I should add, runs from bow to stern, so Hull # 96 is built on 20 major frame members, not counting minor assemblies at bow and transom stern. The loudest noise in the shed this past week has been the big Skilsaw I used to cut the lower floors out of 3/8" sheet stock. I've noticed that not even Paul pesters me while I make the dragon screech.

While most aircraft hulls are circular, ovoid or ellipsoid in cross-section, the real problems in fairing them are at extreme bow and stern sections. They are essentially straight tubes with cones attached. Opposed to this, midship sections of a sailing yacht hull are biradial curves, the bow sections triangular, and stern sections usually diminished versions of what I drew at Station #10.

Lofting is the work of turning lines on a 2' by 3' sheet of paper into the yacht's full dimensions on the loft floor, all 47' 6" of her in this case. Having lofted her, and nearly driven

Steve bats in the process, Earl is masterly calm and wholly in his element, arranging this temple of dinosaur bones above the floor of the big shed. He's even good humored when Tony or I ask him a question, because after this past week he knows we are like him in at least one respect: we are bitten by the bug, and enjoy creating solid geometry in the drafty ethers of Paul's shed.

I've had more than ten minutes of solid boatbuilding data out of Earl today and by watching him have learned vastly more than that. I haven't enjoyed anything so much since I found I was putting the booze locker into *Wandelaar*.

Today Earl had me plumb the stem piece, in between other things, of course. This suggests a certain amount of confidence—to have me actually setting a twelve-foot arc of aluminum, with its attached four frames, into . . . alignment with the rest of the hull. The stem piece, you see, projects well beyond the steel strongback, and . . . must be trued up on its own.

At the whistle tonight, I'd cleaned up and straightened three of the four frames, by use of a giant Tinkertoy arrangement of

Hull ninety-five port-side chain plates, anchors for mast stays. My "master's degree" in welding: Earl had no criticism.

4" aluminum T-stock which defies all . . . logic except maybe that of Archimedes. What this did was fix a big lever, allowing me to gain purchase against the pressure of the frame members.

So what we have is . . . the skeleton of a big beached whale in the shed. And a good chunk of it is my whale, and I like the way it's going together.

. . . . .

And so, apparently, did Earl. As far as I know, number ninety-six put to sea with the bow I gave her. Somehow, that afternoon the squire got his chevrons and sword. It felt that way, then and later. So many years later, it feels that way.

And then it snowed, and the car froze, down to the ground. It was still winter in Maine.

26

The Song of Songs, which Is Stanley's

We sailed with just th' two of us," Stanley remembers, "sometimes three—my uncle would go along." His voice stops, then, gaining memory, "They closed the schools when the flu hit so bad. I was strong for my age, so I went with my father . . ."

He looks up and out and a long way back. "Y'know, there was an outfit at Boston then, owned about fifty schooners workin' along th' coast. There were some big owners then—and a lot o' little outfits, like us. Three and four masters, mostly. We did good durin' th' war—"

The only other sound in the noontime wire shop is the whirring electric heater.

We are sipping a last cup of coffee a few minutes before the whistle calls us back. This is the one room bearable on a day the Montreal Express is beating Linekin Bay to the dark steel of an old gun barrel, flecked with cold white scars. A draft under the west door fills with the pickling sharpness of oak and fresh-cut mahogany ply. Stanley clears his throat, "Hem, but th' bottom fell out, o' course, soon's the war was over.

"Barges could move stuff for near a dollar a ton less, then, an' the' schooner men had t' quit—or go t' bargin' . . . Some did. *We* did, my father and I.

"We managed a few loads out o' Machias, with the schooner, and some lumber from Nova Scotia—" Stanley thinks out loud, matter-of-fact, dryly, his slow periods opening silences he knows his audience will fill. Unless the subject is wood, Stanley in the workday is filled with silence: he will not talk of himself again while I work here.

He offers nothing about what a father and too-young son felt or thought about their winter North Atlantic, about working a slamming brute of a lumber schooner through fog, snow and sleet, past a Gloucester fleet strewn across Georges Bank, just aching eyes to warn them if a doryman could not row clear in time to stay alive; about survival around boom-high stacks of deck-load lumber, a green sea blasting through the only gap giving them access to a peak halyard; about living day and night for a week, shirt freezing to back, lashed in the constant soak of a sailing half-tide rock; trying to work sail with blocks of ice that used to be hands; about whether the donkey engine worked when they had to have it.

Stanley does not talk about wondering, as he struggled forward to ease a sheet, if he ought to have grinned goodbye to his father, who would not see him again until or unless that easing took the terrible roll out of her. Nor about the number of schooners found belly up and their crews gone, when there was time to read a paper at a Quincy lumberyard. Not much time to wonder, working sail: you jump to it, age twelve and a man, and jump again.

Stanley does not talk at all of these things. They were father and son, with his uncle sometimes three, and this vessel was what they were and what they did. Twelve was old enough, and if man-child and man could get this load to Quincy docks or Perth Amboy or Newport, the family would be all right. That is, if the Spanish flu didn't strike at home, while they were out.

The principle was work and the work principal. Neither Mother nor Father spoke of the rest of it, and if they didn't, you didn't. You tailed onto the halyard or heaving line and hauled until you saw Red Hook. Then you went back and did it again.

"But th' paper companies started buyin' up th' mills. So there wasn't any freight atall—took a load of box-boards to Quincy once, to a factory down theah. Coolidge was at Boston, 'twas the police strike, I remember, an' th' National Guard kept everybody movin' right along, if you were walkin' y' couldn't stop anywheres on th' street—not even t' look in a shop window."

"You ever go ashore at South Street, Stanley?"

"Oh, yes . . ." he nods and smiles but doesn't say any more. In that smile, though, in the distant eyes remembering, is the last surge of tides of Stockholm tar, miles of worn manila, furlongs of flying jib booms, garish figureheads, and graying, flaking trailboards; the earth-safe creak of slung-plank fenders against dock piling, draymen cursing, teams lunging under painted ladies gauging a short horizon, and the world and the paint peeling away.

"We did pretty good," Stanley sighs. "We did pretty good from about 1917 to '21. Near everybody went t' steam, then."

The wire room shrinks back to its usual cramped-box shape, and the five of us are quiet a while. Stanley latches his lunchbox, sighs again and closes his eyes. He had come home, we knew, after "everybody went t' steam—" and began building boats at one of the local yards, finally settling in with Paul, where he could work wood among men who respected the work. If you cared about your work, then, you went where you could do it best. Stanley stayed in that path, lifelong.

In some measure that principle lived in what we did, if not always with the quiet focus of Stanley. The rest of us, Earl included, had to work metal when metal was needed. Stanley worked only in wood— had told me only days ago he would do that until somebody had to unclasp his cooling fingers from his jackplane. Steve and I once agreed Stanley must by now have produced enough grab rail to get a sailor hand-over-hand from Kittery to Halifax.

Stanley's habit was to nap a few minutes after lunch on days we let him alone, and he pleased us today with a snore or so, amid the quiet shop talk we finally picked up.

Without seeming ever to hurry, Stanley turned out rods and acres of oak, spruce, fir, mahogany and teak, billows of butternut, a favorite hardwood under sharp hand-tools. He would borrow Tony or myself to help him lift teak plank out of timber storage below the bandsaw, then onto his long bench next door. In a few days, he would call us both off to help him move forty feet of teak toe rail on board a hull. Later, with varnish on, we had to lay nose-to-surface to see the joining. On one hull, a big plank with a buried defect split free of its midship clamps before its lag bolts could be tightened. It took Stanley a day to repair, and the repair was stronger than the original wood: he faired in a block longer than the break. The grain matched. With varnish on, the joins were invisible.

In solitary partnership at his bench, Stanley's planes and spokeshaves whispered steadily through his wood, the shapes turning fluid as shavings piled up at his feet, then flowed like music to pattern and form. Watching him was as good as listening to Vivaldi, and Tony, Steve and I made detours just to pass his bench when he was shaping wood. In my months of practice at Paul's, I never saw Stanley hammer anything into place. If a trial didn't fit, he paced his quiet measuring dance until it did, without fuss or fume, eye-smooth and hand-soft, part of the whole sculpture of the boat.

Without trying to adjust anyone's attitude, he showed us ideas that led us to good work. He could probably do it faster alone but was never impatient with us wanting to understand wood or woodwork. We could all make a required shape, but Stanley could make that shape breathe.

Among the joiners Earl was quicker than any. As foreman, interrupted constantly by Paul and all his younger joiners, Earl's dynamo speed overawed all but Stanley and our employer. A quality equal to Stanley's flew from that perpetual gale, but not with Stanley's music.

Looking at Earl's work, your mind had to say, *That's right*. Looking at Stanley's work, your heart understood, *Of course*.

The whistle moved us from bench and chair and battery case. Stanley waked, age seventy-five, smiling upward toward the skylight, brightening now as a moment of sun worked through the noontime cloud and cold.

Luke Yard, October 1978, a warm noon; Tom Sr., machinist (left), and Stanley Mitchell, reflective.

27

Wear Your Own Gloves

May 9, 1979, the Luke Yard: On my knees in the shed doorway gasping for breath, I clutched my wrist. Young Tom wrapped my right hand in a towel. My planet condensed itself to a small hope that the hand I couldn't look at was repairable, and a lesser hope that I could faint or hit some other part of myself so hard that it would distract from the outrage at the end of my right arm. I stamped on the floor. It didn't help.

Over my head was a murmur; then young Tom and another man eased me up, one on each side, and got me up the parking lot into Tom's car, where I promptly tried to kick a hole in the floor, just to feel some other hurt beyond my hand. I remember wanting to tell Tom why I was doing this, but don't know that I actually got words out. Tom drove me to St. Andrews at the Harbor, carefully and fast. I have no memory of the drive, beyond Tom trying to say soothing things. And then we were in the ER, and a nurse was getting me on a gurney, coaxing my left hand away from my right. I didn't dare look at the hand, even wrapped up. The doctor was there in moments, ordered a local anesthetic, and went to work.

* * *

Wearing borrowed welding gauntlets, I had taken a small aluminum plate to the metal brake on that May afternoon. The plate was to become part of the cabin coach roof on hull number ninety-six. The brake had adjustable rolls, to create a smooth bend in any piece you fed it, but the right glove fingertips were a little long. My right-hand fingers went into the roll beneath the plate. I remember surprise as my hand pulled me toward the brake—and my left hand on the reversing switch, jamming it hard over before the pain drove me to my knees. I didn't see the coach roof on number ninety-six for another month and then only for the little while it took to shake hands with the gang, which by then I was happy to be able to do, carefully, with my repaired right hand. Paul told me I was welcome, he'd be glad to have me back. But the injury, the scare, and the month of thinking time all combined to convince me my apprentice time was done, at least in Paul's yard. I needed to see what I could do somewhere else.

My ability to focus on work improved by light-years. Since that afternoon, I've had just two minor power-tool injuries and very few hand-tool slips, all minor. To me it is a given that a tool I do not pay attention to will injure me at some point in its or my work, and the worst injury will come from the tool—edged or not—that I do not properly set up and maintain. And I am very careful to buy work gloves that fit.

My luck arrives at awkward times. The surgeon at St. Andrews Hospital that warm May afternoon was not distracted when I chanted pieces of *Jabberwocky*, while he worked on my hand. He was amused, patient, calm even, when I yelled once, sure that he was taking off the worst finger. He had interned at Bellevue in Manhattan, he said, and then stayed through his surgical residency. He long since had seen most of the damage we do ourselves and each other and was not dismayed by mere mashed fingers. The roll had caught the first two fingers on my hand and then rolled them back out again when I hit the reverse switch. He told me I had pretty well flayed the first finger down to the second knuckle but only squished my second finger. According to the X-ray, it looked as if all the kneaded joints were still there: a miracle.

His nurse held my left hand and tended the anesthetic and let me respond to the doctor's, "I want you to—just a little bit—wiggle your index finger," and "Can you feel that? Try your second finger. OK." Over a couple of hours, he cleaned up and closed up the index finger, neatly sewing the damaged parts of both digits, talked with his patient and his nurse, told me enough about his Bellevue experience to assure me he knew what he was doing, and finally told Tom, sitting patiently nearby, that he could take me home. By this time it may have been a tad past four o'clock. Tom and the doctor had asked me long since if I wanted the hospital to call Barbara. I was aware enough to know that Barbara could leap to anxiety in nothing flat, so I made the announcement myself, walking toward her from where Tom parked his car at the foot of the lawn. Staggering, in fact, I'd needed a more-than-ordinary amount of anesthetic to dull the hand, and the juice now was in charge. Tom and Barbara aimed me at the living-room couch. After listening to Tom and then to me, she seemed to relax a little. I think I napped, and then Steve and tall, lanky Bill-the-Wire showed up, bringing my car, to see how the patient was doing. We talked long enough so they heard that the doctor had said I was to go back to his surgery the next day, and it would probably be some weeks before I could work safely.

Next day, after the doctor inspected and rewrapped his needlework, I phoned Paul. He listened and finally said, "Well, take the time you need to mend. But I hope you'll come back, soon's you can. We've got a lot o' work in." I wasn't sure that I could or would, but his asking was a real comfort just then.

* * *

My IBM typewriter from 1967 sat on a folding table in our apartment kitchen. From earlier tries, I knew I would get out little more than a few lines if we moved back to my mother's place. The only spot available there would be the middle of all the traffic through her house, and Mother had many friends in the village.

Since September I'd spent some part of each evening trying to make a story of my days in the yard, beginning with bits culled from letters exchanged with my father in August. Somehow preserved through three serious changes of address, a few rags of those early pages came with us, wind-waffle philosophizing, ideas pecking back and forth like free-range hens, hectic notions bouncing off something deeper that looked far too much like a white whale. I've admired Melville ever since I discovered his journey with Ishmael and Ahab in a discarded issue of Classic Illustrated comics, and on a restless evening I can still gladly browse my treasured Lakeside Press volume, three years older than its reader.

But at Boothbay, in that spring of '79, all horizons were suddenly hazy, and the only location flexible enough to let me find work, perhaps even better pay, would involve going home, to test once more my mother's hospitality and patience. While Barbara and I talked over possibilities, the mail brought our introduction to Maine Worker's Compensation insurance, when Paul's wife had sent along the papers needed to file a disability claim. As a basic greeting from The System, the claim process in the late 70s was designed to discourage claimants from sloughing off the Protestant work ethic for any reason short of dismemberment. I filed but within a month knew I would keep the use of my fingers and hand so cancelled my claim after getting one or two truly modest checks. And the world, almost at once, began to look less grim.

The doctor's reassembly and his little blue handball-to-squeeze did all he hoped they would. While I was on the gurney that afternoon, he said, "It looks like it lined up all right, and you may even keep the nail. But how much use you get back is up to you. So start flexing all the fingers on that hand as soon as you can and for as long as you can stand. Nerves are funny, and you could end up with the rest of your fingers stiff unless you keep them all in motion every day."

I still wanted to build boats, but other things had to happen first.

By 1978 I'd spent enough of my life working for a paycheck and needed to work for several things not pursued in boardrooms, banks, or belligerence. A modest miracle had given me time to read a book by James Krenov, mentioned earlier, whose practical philosophy still makes great good sense to me. Following Krenov's thread through a maze at first invisible, I had arrived in a few months to Ocean Point and Paul E. Luke, Inc., where, judging by the result, I lost my mind entirely for the time reflected in my story. And perhaps for life: I still enjoy boat work. But we moved inland once more, while I healed. I've learned since that one is not easily healed of a true possession. I am still possessed by boats and the sea to this day.

Now, to close the circle you need to know a little more about Steve and Tony.

28

Steve, Apprentice, Master (June 1999)

By late afternoon on this June Friday, most of the yard crew had gone home. About twenty years after we last compared sprains, spavins and history at Paul's, I found Steve Zimmerman on foot near his yard launching slip, at the edge of Chesapeake Bay. As I turned the shed corner, Steve stooped to collect a bit of scrap and tossed this into a discreet trash barrel. My friend still liked things neat. He smiled and shook hands. Sunburned and slim, Steve to me looked young as he had at Boothbay, his age only in his higher forehead and close-clipped hair, beginning to gray at the temples. Jackson-dog, big, black and amiable, ranged wagging back and forth as we ambled up the yard toward Steve's office. On the front porch rail were posted rules for visitors:

1. Come in and walk around the shops and look closely at our work. We fired the insurance company that said we couldn't let our customers and visitors into our shops.
2. Ask us questions. We are proud of what we do here and would enjoy talking to you about our work.
3. Walk freely around the yard and have a look at the fine yachts we have the opportunity to work on.

My memory of Steve at Paul's was of a thin, intensely focused young man, whose working expression most of the time ranged from mild concern to fierce frustration. That look is gone. The good-humored eyes are calm, a little speculative. It's been a long while; they reasonably think, Who is this man now? His eyes are so steady over the remembered voice that I ask if he does a meditation practice.

"Aikido," he says. "I've been a student for eight years, and I teach a class now in Mathews, once a week." He explains that aikido is an essentially defensive martial art, borrowing from the disciplines of judo, karate, and kendo, for the dual purposes of self-discipline and self-defense. It is based on the use of an opponent's own energy to disarm or weaken him and is often called the spiritual martial art. Steve will go Saturday to northern Virginia for a scheduled class with his teacher, and he thinks of himself as a lifetime student.

He needs to clear up some paper and phone calls. I go out and stroll around the clean, quiet yard. There are no jumbled piles of discarded blocking, no ranges of waste barrels, no shed-side scree slopes of debris, at least in the main yard. Most of the yachts from winter storage are in the bay and gone; a few stand near the spare, neat, closed sheds occasionally set off by cared-for clumps of pine and some deciduous trees I can't identify. Steve stores and maintains sail and power yachts. One or two are still in the storage lot beyond the sheds, three boats (two sailing auxiliaries and a power cruiser) are cradled on stands near the grove of lanky pine separating his shore yard from the big inland storage lot. It has been so long since I trolled the ads in any yachting magazine that I can't identify the builder of any of the three. Later I learn they will go in the water on Saturday.

I'm dazed by the abrupt contrast between this quiet sundown shore and my previous five days, spent with my old friend Ed Mickey and his Ruth. Ed, a builder of classical pipe organs, had asked me to help move him from rural central Maine into a North Carolina mountain garden. After a week of long-haul rush and thunder down a highway, here is peace, birdsong, and a showcase for the only industry I ever fell in love with.

Ed has just started for his new home after driving me across much of North Carolina and a huge wedge of Virginia. It is all strange country, and here I stand on the edge of legendary Chesapeake Bay. Steve's yard is so neat it looks like a stage set, and my photos agree with this. This effect will vanish when his crew arrive Saturday morning; all will be bustle and purpose again. But for these evening hours, it seems somehow too neat to be a working yard.

I look at surfaces and am oddly pleased with the sight and sound of the gravel underfoot, then step into the office and find Steve is done with his work.

We talk as he leads me through his building sheds, remembering.

Steve is younger than myself by enough years to have sharp memories of his first days at the Luke yard. Knowing him then and now, there could have been no question of his commitment, his rocket learning curve, or his high energy. But what Paul wanted to know first was, Will He Stay? Steve's first assignment on Ocean Point was a keg of aluminum wing nuts. These Paul wanted drilled and tapped (threaded for their matching bolts). He took Steve to the machine shop and a drill press. The keg of wing nuts stood on one side, an empty fifty-five-gallon drum on the other. Paul showed Steve the steps he must follow to get a clean, threaded product and then went away for a half hour.

And returned, to say, "You're not goin' fast enough!" These regular visits and protests continued until Paul was satisfied that Steve's pace was at least adequate. Steve doesn't remember the number of visits, just the exasperation of them, at least that first day, probably on succeeding days. It took him two or three days to complete the drilling and tapping. By the time Steve finished, he felt pretty good about his speed. He found Paul and told him the wing nuts were done. Paul said, "Well, bring 'em ovuh heah—" and led him to an inch-wide belt sander set up on a nearby bench.

Paul showed Steve how to turn the wing nuts against the belt, to remove all the casting ridges left by the mold, "Got that?"

"Yeah!" Steve settled into what he thought was a useful sanding routine. As before, Paul returned every half-hour, "You're not goin' fast enough!" And the visits continued. Finally, he was done with the wing nuts, but only at cost of fingers sore from continual cuts and abrasions. It was almost impossible to rotate the wing nuts against that narrow belt with gloves on, so he did most of the sanding bare-handed, in a hurry.

Paul next led him out to the big shed, handed him an industrial disc sander, picked up another and showed him the process for grinding mill scale off aluminum plate. The average size plate was four foot by twelve foot. This doesn't sound especially big until you are alone and want to turn it over to sand the other side. Then you learn about the chain fall and how long it takes to set a C-clamp, lift the sheet and turn it over. After which you grind away at the second side.

Building custom yacht hulls from aluminum, you begin to see that all of this takes a great deal of time, that this time equals money, and that profit disappears unless everybody does his work at the best speed possible. Not the fastest. The best. Sanding scale off aluminum plate is one of the less immediately rewarding jobs in Christendom and one at which a bright young apprentice may soon wilt and endure some degree of pain. The position is that used in planting a rice paddy, with the added attraction of keeping a two-handed grip on about ten to twelve pounds of whirling disc sander/grinder at arms' length, while you swing it in a repeated wide arc, pivoting from your hips, grinding at foot level. This pattern of motion becomes your life, is accompanied by the high-speed howl of the grinder motor and its complaining bearings, and if you live long enough, the four o'clock whistle may send you home.

After ten minutes of this, the glamour of creating seagoing sculpture dims. Distinct from the paddy work, of course, your feet are dry. Only your head is bubbling. If you live through this, you are building boats—big, beautiful boats. If you are still there after a couple of weeks, you very likely have the full classic set of signs and symptoms: your back hurts; your eye kindles at the mention of technique; your mate, partner or significant other does not comprehend much of your speech; and you cannot wait to try out your idea tomorrow morning, at a time when sane people are rolling over for another nap or making sure the coffee is actually perking.

Steve's back grew strong, his patience and skills growing with it. Paul decided he would make him a joiner and kept him on, finally to the day when he was sure Steve ought to help Bill Fagan run wire in the current boat. All this took place a year before I heard Paul's name.

Only if you have sailed in a boat where stray current was melting fastenings out of the leaking hull can you know how crucial this decision was. Saltwater is an electrolyte. Give it voltage to carry and it will, cheering all the way. Whole keels have fallen off boats where the wire was left ungrounded. A boat that does not over time disassemble itself is not an accident. Somebody took hellacious pains with that wire, so you would live another day. Bow toward mecca, this is nothing you earned. This only happens if the electrician has a boss sensitive to priorities and detail and if the man or woman putting the details in place is determined to get them right.

Zimmerman Marine has a product, one that Steve has thought about, conjured with, meditated on, arranged schedules for, produced, and delivered for several of the eighteen years he has been his own boss. His yard's nominal product—apart from storage, maintenance, repair and commissioning of boats—is a sturdy family motor cruiser, designed around and built into the classic Maine lobsterman hull. The hull in fact is built in Maine and then shipped to Steves' Mobjack Bay yard for fitting to client needs and druthers. The result of months of critical attention to details of shape, proportion, machinery, and utility is as nearly immaculate a motor yacht as an owner can have in its size range, thirty-six feet. It is substantial, as products go, but it is, like every boat built here, strictly an expression of the tangible product of this place.

The tangible product. It has been written about before, probably better. It is called "quality," and a more intelligent consideration of it can be found in *Zen and the Art of Motorcycle Maintenance*, written by Robert Pirsig.

"Quality is that without which a thing is not itself," according to Noah Webster and friends. The definition compresses the idea, but not by much.

The ancient Anglo-Saxon words are *yare* and *trig*, and the completed work I see in the yard is yare and trig. Steve has cause to look calm and composed. His people, from what I see of jobs in hand, appreciate that there is a galaxy beyond neat and workmanlike. The result, even to my sleep-deprived eye, shows up in the several boats being built or repaired. Care is taken with lines and edges; the wood has a softer shape where a body can hit it; the varnish is deep where the sun and water will strike; the paint surfaces are flawless. Underneath, wire is channeled in neat runs, and the fit of piping is clean as the fit of wood.

A New Jersey native, Steve at the University of Virginia pursued a combined major of psychology, political theory, and religious studies, probably unique in the annals of boatbuilding. He had been accepted into the university's law school, when in 1977 he helped deliver the yacht *Rosa* to her builder, Paul Luke of East Boothbay. Steve was stricken, and the law lost a scholar and probable jurist soon after Paul handed him that first wing nut. Steve grins at me, shedding the years between then and now; it was, he says, "I gotta build a boat! I just gotta build a boat!"

Surviving all the trials of the afflicted, Steve absorbed everything he could in the Luke shops and then went looking for more experience in wooden-boat construction. That under his belt, he borrowed from an interested friend, found the Mobjack Bay site, already equipped with a modest marine railway, and signed the lease. He was twenty-seven, a skilled builder but lacking in business training. After two years he struck a reef common enough in business startups: there was not enough money coming in to keep on. He could build a fine boat but never had studied business or management.

After a night spent thinking his way from realization to urgent recovery, Steve began a search for advice and partners to help him design a plan to market his yard and skills. He found partners skilled in business, marketing and banking, and the result worked increasingly well until the following spring, when lightning struck.

Delivering *Rosa* to City Island that spring, he met and admired a handsome Mathis-Trumpy motor yacht, whose owner in turn admired *Rosa*. Learning that Steve's yard maintained *Rosa*, *Enticer*'s owner asked Steve to create the same artful work for him. Not long after, *Enticer* met *Sequoia*, a larger Mathis-Trumpy then owned by the Presidential Yacht Trust, whose members were impressed. With *Sequoia*'s fame and her successful restoration, the yard drew national media attention, all to good effect. By 1987 only nine years after leaving Luke's, Steve and his advisors and partners had a solvent business and that most valuable business asset, word-of-mouth advertising. Karl Muller produced the Zimmerman yard's incentive program, rewarding staff for productivity and high quality, and Haywood May, boatbuilder and liveaboard cruiser, then President of Bass Harbor Marine, coupled the knowledge gained in his life to that in Steve's operation.

As a sort of benison, a European yachtsman who summered on Mobjack Bay contracted in 1992 for Steve and his crew to build *Chanty*. A wishbone ketch fifty-two feet overall, designed by Bruce King, her hull cold molded, the yacht took two years to complete. She promptly graced the covers of *Chesapeake Bay*, *WoodenBoat* and *Yachting* magazines and continues to draw admiring reviews. Although I've seen only drawings and photos, I feel safe in adding another: *Chanty* is in boatbuilding a poem aligning sense, design, and fine building.

Great risk. Great reward. In a trade with a high rate of early business mortality, Steve and his people built a success on their faith that there are and will be men and women who want and will buy graceful, strong, loveable, and long-lived boats.

After finding me a bunk for the night, Steve fixes a spaghetti-and-salad meal, at which his son Ian joins us. Ian is anxious to be out with friends, so we eat rather than talk, and I ride with Steve and Ian to where he will meet the other boys. Steve's wife, Gwen, and daughter, Rachel, are away until late evening. We trade a couple of stories about our mutual time at East Boothbay and the things we learned there, about the work and about ourselves. We are sleepy and have an early day Saturday, so do not stay up.

In the early light, sheds and trees have soft edges, and only the moored boats have character. With sunup, the swallows dance through trees, rigging and dock pilings, gathering a bug breakfast. I eat with Steve, and he goes to his office a few minutes before we leave for Woodbridge, where I can find a northbound train. Steve will go on to Falls Church for a class with his aikido sensei teacher of eight years. He will come back to Cardinal, practice, and teach others this art without weapons, in the belief that this practice can help others toward a life less stressful, more focused, and better balanced. His teaching is part of his apprenticeship, and in an evening and a morning I've heard a little of his practice applied, as he spoke with one or another man in the yard. Boats were launched Saturday morning before we left, as soon as the crew assembled: the lack of drama surprised me, after what I had seen and done at Paul's.

Respected as employer, manager and workman, Steve had assembled and orchestrated a crew intent on producing quality as a matter of course. But—dependable high quality is not and never has been a matter of course. It is a candle out there in the dark, just visible at the outer edge of hope, arrived at by your own mix of hope and prayer, focus and genius, vision and work. You have to believe in it, before you can set a course toward it, and trust that you will see the rocks and shoals in time to find a safe passage. And remember there are people out there who believe as you do, whether or not they can talk about it in words you understand. There are, usually, just enough of them to keep you alive along your way. You will still have to fight for it.

We shook hands one more time at the Amtrak station in Woodbridge, Virginia. Steve drove off waving. Inside at the ticket booth, I found the Amtrak northbound express did not run on Saturday. I sat in the shade and read about Irish poets until a Trailways coach showed up, northbound.

29

Tony Now, Ocean Point, East Boothbay, c. 2000

Working for Paul, I sometimes imagined the way a home and shop by the ocean ought to look. When I found Tony and his wife, they were arranging the garden between my imagined shop and home. They lived in this millennium year on Wall Street, a gravel lane far friendlier than the Manhattan money canyon.

A gent named Bill, at the little restaurant on the wharf in East Boothbay, knew exactly where Tony would be on a sunny spring afternoon. I followed Ocean Point Road, then Van Horn, watching for Wall, which led me directly to Linekin Bay Woodworkers, Inc. There was just room for a couple of cars off the lane, then the shop, a garden, a cape that doesn't seem big enough to hold husband, wife and four energetic boys age ten to eighteen.

When I asked if Tony Jose lived here, Mrs. Jose, directing agriculture, pointed at her husband and vanished toward the house. I'd interrupted what in Maine amounts to the holiest rite of spring, planting the vegetable beds. This happens much sooner on the coast than inland, and when wife and husband collaborate, I'm inclined to be trepid about intruding on the ceremony. (Myself wed to a gardener for forty years, I just dig where she points. This seems to work.) But I did intrude. It had been a long time.

Tony is patient today as he was while I was ruining his work shirts with my welding, is even bigger and taller than I recall, and is happy to show me his shop and his albums of past work. He is a little less reserved than the man with the boy's face that I remember, but without effort he still looks young.

The most impressive thing is, Joseph Anthony Jose looks like a man at peace with himself, with his life and work. The human race once claimed this was characteristic of wise simplicity, or maybe I was young, and imagined that. In any event, the result shows in Tony's work, which looks clean and simple, until you begin to count curves and glass and items of detailing that require huge amounts of time, energy, planning, order, and patience to do cleanly and "simply."

I asked if his boys helped in the shop. His grin was answer enough, "No, they're all into academics, all plan to go to college." Leafing through acres of kitchens, renovations, case work and table work, yacht cabins ranging from Spartan and formal to a recent major installation—the owner's stateroom in *Antonisa*, a mega yacht launched from Tim Hodgdon's yard in the fall of 1999. This I'd seen during summer of '99, when Kennebec Valley Woodworkers Association (a regional guild of independent Maine woodworkers) had the pleasure of a guided tour, shortly before *Antonisa* left her building shed. Richly photographed for *Down East* and *WoodenBoat*, the pictures suggest but can't reveal the jaw-dropping wealth of workmanship devoted to fitting out deck work and accommodation. You may remember it was a younger Tony, not Earl or Stanley, who made sure more than once that my joints in cabin furniture for *Wandelaar* and *Tempting* passed the microscope test.

At least fifty-five first-rank joiners labored on *Antonisa* between 1995 and her launch in 1999, and it showed. The quality throughout was easily as high as that I'd seen in *Yachting* magazine photos from the late 20s and 30s in the grandest of grand luxury yachts of that era. At the time of the KVWA, visit I had not known Tony was building part of the boat. Men not given to much praise simply stood or revolved slowly in the owner's stateroom, nodding.

Tony still favors the short sentence, but uses more of them than when we tacked plate on *Tempting*. He had been a year at Luke's when I signed on in August '78. He wed his fiancée that month and stayed on with Earl for five years, before he struck out on his own. It was as near a classical apprentice term as one could have in that time, and Tony absorbed principles, technique, and practice from Earl, Stanley, and all others since, judging by the work he has done. "I just stayed here on the Gold Coast, John," he smiled, explaining. "We built this place as we went along, and I did whatever anyone needed done."

And with that quality of work, the word of course spread. "I finally had four men on full-time, but it got crazy. I wanted the woodwork and time with the kids. It's easier working alone. I did some shows for a while, but not anymore."

We strolled outside toward my truck; I was anxious not to take up his garden time. In the first balmy afternoon in far too long after an endless winter, Linekin Bay smelled sweet in the breeze off the water. Three of the boys whizzed by on bikes, smiling.

Tony remembered something. "You know Earl is gone?"

"Yes, cancer I heard."

"Yeah, not long after he retired from Luke's. A while after the funeral, I got a call from Mrs. Dodge. She wanted me to come see her. I think it was a few weeks after Earl died. So I went in, and she sat me down and gave me a lecture on shop ventilation and chemicals, dust masks and shop safety. She wanted me to take care of my health, generally.

"And then she gave me all of Earl's hand-tools."

He smiled and we shook hands. "Come again," he said and went back to the garden. I was still smiling when I got home.

30

Generations, 1 July 2001

At the driveway off Ocean Point Road is a sheriff's car. Standing by it is a slim, older man, his uniform immaculate in the late-morning heat. He confirms that I have the right driveway, his eyes amused in a face I'd think more likely seen explaining why a term paper needs more editing.

Two dozen or so polished sedans are parked in the yard's shady spots, among them a crimson Corvette and a restored early woody beach wagon. Cars are following me, so I tuck the War Wagon, my aging small truck, in where no one will brain himself on the sea kayak it carries, pick up my camera and follow a much older couple in blazer and sun hat, slowly around to the shore side of the shed row. I hear folks have come from Florida for the event. It is Sunday, 1 July 2001, the date set by the family at Paul's death for a gathering to honor his work and life.

Drinks are set up in the shade of the roll-around shelter. In the shed bay, where years ago we raised scaffold around *Sea Swallow*, tables are heavy with food and soft drinks. A small stage at the head of this bay holds a floral tribute, wild flowers and tame, native to Paul's shore, a grace note from the owners and crew of *Rosa II*, in memory of their long, hectic, affectionate relationship with Paul and his people.

At noon the crowd grows quickly. Age more than youth at first, with most hair white or absent, male faces ruddy, liver spots like merit badges on the eldest, a lot of the senior clothing yacht-club formal. Among the curling eddies of elder conversation, the next generation begins to thicken, many in slacks or shorts, sport shirts, sandals, a rucksack here and there. Some have brought children, from teens to toddler. By age and inclination, the kids soon find each other and go exploring in what is still Paul's version of Merlin's Cave, the sheds.

At the yard moorings are several Luke boats sailed specially to this day's event, and berthed at the dock float is a neat, small schooner in bright finish. The first Luke I find is Frank, now managing the yard, but Frank is deep among friends and clients, so I wander on, looking for John Luke. Approaching a man studying the crowd from near the marine railway, I find he is David Clarke, owner and builder of the admired schooner.

He is looking for his wife Nancy, who planned to drive over from New Hampshire today. David spots John Luke for me and in the same breath invites me for a guided tour of his boat. He is here today because the Lukes, especially Frank, have been for him a continual source of encouragement and technical advice over the years he and Nancy spent building their schooner. Eighteen years, he says. I promise I will come to the boat as soon as I make my manners. Until Chip Luke steps up to take the microphone, I keep looking for Verna, Paul's widow. She appears with a friend in tow, as Chip welcomes the hundred and more assembled around the floral table and stage.

On behalf of the family, Chip welcomes all and introduces Roger Duncan and a second friend, who speak in turn, warmly, of Paul, his genius as a fine builder and lifelong friend, and of his family. Roger Duncan is the living spirit and chief compiler of *A Cruising Guide to the New England Coast*, steadily in print since 1937. Duncan looks painfully thin, frail and tired, but his firm, clear voice carries well against the breeze. He and Paul were friends for years, but somehow his compact history misses the mixture of instant invention, mischief, short fuse, tireless work, and raucous laughter that made Paul the only charismatic builder I ever met. The old gentleman's respect and affection for Paul are vivid, but in his talk the combustible character doesn't get past the genius who helped energize the building of an amazing number of yard tugs in WWII at Sample's Boatyard in nothing flat. I look down to find flaming red hair and freckles about four years old standing at my feet, smiling straight up at me in beatitude so perfect I have to smile back. He has wrapped a string attached to his grandsire—seated a little in front of where I stand at the shed wall—around his camouflage fatigue outfit. While I watch, he gently revolves back through standees to grandfather, carefully drawing himself along, a dance that pleases both of them and me, too.

I miss the second speaker's name and part of his comment about Paul's genius for inventing his way along; then Chip is up again to thank all for coming to honor his grandsire's life and to invite everyone to stay and enjoy the picnic the family has set up on the shed tables. The crowd moves in a smooth wave toward the food, mostly away from the wine and beer. Friends gather a plate and break away to talk, while Frank, John, Chip, and several Luke women chat with different groups.

Today the family all wear blue knit shirts with the Luke logo. A little awed at the number of these—in 1978 I was aware only of Frank and John as Paul's and Verna's children—I lose count at about a dozen shirts. Suddenly finding Chip alone, I introduce myself and he grins. "You'd have been here just before I showed up. Soon's I was old enough, he was on my case."

I tell Chip how useless I felt in my first weeks at the yard, and his grin broadens, "Wasn't he a bear to work for? I think I can find a note penciled here on the wall for every year of my life, a piece of work he wanted me to do, a reminder 'case I didn't do it the way he wanted. I've never worked for a tougher boss, nor expect to." This is paraphrase, of course. We are surrounded by gossip, good cheer, and a mélange of vocal noise my ears will no longer usefully separate. As to family and durability, it takes less than five minutes with Chip to persuade me that Paul engraved every essential in Frank's oldest son before Alzheimer's forced them apart. Better, Paul and Frank made sure Chip looked at things with his own eyes and seem to have left him with small taste for untested wisdom—a good start for a young builder.

"Invent what you need. Here, try this. You can do it faster this way, and better. Are ye gainin' on it?"

A visitor in the shop wonders out loud what Paul would think if he saw designs and lofting laid out by computer these days. Chip takes a deep breath and says, "He would have been the first man on the coast with a CAD/CAM setup. He was a leader, and he rubbed people raw sometimes, but he led. He got the job done and the work out."

Chip grins again, "Somebody asked him if it wasn't hard to see these beautiful boats go down the bay. Paul told him no, he was running a business, and he didn't get his check until the boat sailed."

Romance my arse, I have to meet a payroll! I can hear Paul thinking the words he would seldom say to anyone but crew. "Godsake, cover the cost. Give me a dime to grow on." Being in charge is an isolating job at both ends, a point the MBA mills discuss quietly, if at all. It is a transforming experience to look a good man in the eye while you hand him his last check and tell him he is laid off indefinitely. Most of us need body armor to think of discharging good people, taking their living away from them, let alone actually doing it.

We find Lyn Smith, most patient of welders. Rounding up Billy, we manage a reunion photograph with John Luke and Tom, who worked at Paul's during and just after my own time.

I find a sandwich and amble down the dock, a little way behind David Clarke and his Nancy, just arrived. My impression of the Clarke schooner is a compact and wonderfully neat fisherman hull, carefully detailed to maintain character. She is dressed in a surprising amount of practical/ornamental brass and bronze work, crowned with an opulent mermaid supporting the binnacle, a statue from classical lost-wax molding. David created the mold himself from a richly carved table pedestal, and a sculptor friend did the bronze foundry work and casting.

More evidence of eighteen years' work is below decks. At an early stage in building, David came across an old steam yacht, the hull hogged from years on dry land in a bad cradle, badly set. Hoping at first to salvage her complete, he approached the owners and began dickering.

David said, "Then I got a look at how bad the hull was, so we finally got her for not much, if we would promise to leave nothing behind but cleared land. They wanted her out and the shed down. We did that after we got most everything above deck off her—just got the local fire department to use it for a training exercise. But everything above that deck was Andaman padauk, from 1909, and we were able to save most of it for the finish you see here."

The finish here gleams many shades of red, as if lights flare inside the wood. James Krenov writes of an ancient log of Andaman padauk discovered in a lumberyard shed near his home in Sweden. He makes it sound like poetry. Now I can see why he was so pleased.

Over that eighteen years, David and Nancy found and preserved brass and bronze, wood carvings from France and Japan, light fixtures from early twentieth-century yachts and fishermen. It was shared work, through bad times and good, and the result a live-in work of art, able under sail over long ocean passages. The schooner nearly divided them once, then rejoined them, Nancy explained, when they found neither was whole without the other and their beautiful long-range home.

Maybe it was all that luminous padauk. The boat's interior, finally, gave me the feeling I might have if I could visit friends inside a beating heart. We issued mutual invitations to visit and shook hands for quite a while, and I found my shoes and went ashore before my eye glasses could fog up any worse.

*   *   *

And that is the yard and my story. I had spent a fall, winter, and spring building boats and parts of boats, as one of a crew like none I've known before or since, for a man who could roar outrage and be intentionally funny in the same breath.

To me the saddest thing of all is Paul's end. Tragic enough for the man or woman diagnosed with it, Alzheimer's is equally a tragedy for all who must deal with it and with the afflicted friend or family member. I think in this case it took away a genius. A genius for any work is surely magic, but a genius for good, strong, faithful boats is somewhere beyond magic. Not many have it.

To have been cut away from this at the peak of his ability is a kind of insult that makes one doubt the value of belief systems, let alone the goodness of God. To what do we owe such an end? But it happens. With a little luck, most of us leave some good thing behind. Paul Luke did that and more. Paul left a standard of workmanship; he created a bank of skills, and he made room—and allowances—for apprentice work.

I live inland now, near a lake. I work wood, some of it boat wood, paddle a sea kayak I surely overbuilt. My slim boat, *Leaf*, likes to stay right side up. Paul and his people taught me good things. Few days go by that I do not use some skill I first practiced on Ocean Point, and Paul, Earl, and Stanley are with me still, face and voice, years later, as vivid as the day I last saw them.

Appendix

Letter from John Gardner

A four-page blessing, complete with helpful comment, from the man then in charge of Mystic Seaport Museum's Small Craft Collection and it s preservation. Himself a writer and philosopher and lifelong lover of small boats, John Gardner wrote for *Maine Coast Fisherman* and *National Fisherman*. Among his works is *Building Classic Small Craft: Complete Plans and Instructions for 47 Boats*. John later sent me written permission to use his letter and comments on what then went under *Journal* as a working title. What he had was a hasty and even Godawful badly typed and scribbled-over first draft. Anyway, you can see why I subsequently burnt up my Selectric with further drafts.

---

18 Mistuxet Ave.
Mystic, Conn. 06355
July 11, 1984

John H. Willey
RDF 1, Box 3560
Pinewood Point
Mt. Vernon, Me 04352

Dear John:

When I said it might take me awhile before I read your Journal, I never thought it would take this long. Finally, last night after supper I sat down with it, and didn't get up until I had finished, about 2 AM. I have to say that some of it I skimmed through, but not your account

18 Mistuxet Ave.
Mystic, Conn. 06355
July 11, 1984

John H. Willey
RFD 1, Box 3560
Pinewood Point
Mt. Vernon, Me. 04352

Dear John:

When I said it might take me awhile
before I read your Journal, I never thought
it would take this long. Finally, last night
after supper I sat down with it, and didn't
get up until I had finished, about 2 AM.
I have to say that some of it I skimmed
through, but not your account of your
"apprentice Ship" with Paul Luke. That was
something else. The shop, and crew, and
Paul came through life size. I was there
with you, every blessed, excruciating, wonderful
minute.

Paul needed help bad, you said you were a
joiner, they said: "We'll find out." That funny
little Jap saw, no tool chest, no butt gudge,
no back saw, no two-foot rule.—Odear Odear
Ohdear". I know exactly how the Baron felt.
But you tried, and you worked, and you
must have produced. And then one day you
got mad and a shouting match with the boss
ensued. That was when you made it,

of your "apprenticeship" with Paul Luke. That was something else.
The shop, and crew, and Paul came through life size. I was there with
you, every blessed, excruciating, wonderful minute.

Paul needed help bad, you said you were a joiner, they said: "We'll
find out." That funny little Jap saw, no tool chest, no butt gauge, no
back saw, no two-foot rule—Odear Odear Odear." I know exactly how
the Baron felt.* But you tried, and you worked, and you must have
produced. And then one day you got mad and a shouting match with
the boss ensued. That was when you made it.

* The term "Baron" refers to Earl Dodge, the joiner foreman.

I had a shouting match with the boss once, myself. It works, that is if you are really mad enough and have the right kind of a boss.

Did I tell you that long ago I was a boatyard apprentice, myself at the age of 35 in 1940 when I signed on as a planker at the James E. Groves yard in Marblehead at the beginning of World War II? True, as a boy on the St. Croix River at Calais, Maine, I had watched, and had helped boat builders some. In Maine in those days a boy naturally picked up some wood working skill—it was part of growing up, but that didn't make them boat builders, not by a long shot.

After boyhood came normal school, teaching, graduate work at Columbia, the Movement (Fourth International) organizing unem-

3

Mystic Seaport 15 years ago, at Fred
Dion's yard in Salem, Massachusetts.

Fred was the same breed as Paul Luke,
and ran the same kind of yard, except
that he specialized in servicing and
repairing fine wooden yachts, building
very few. The same kind of joiner shop,
the same sort of crew, but no Baron.
Fred was his own Baron. Fred and I
got along fine. Would give me a job and
leave me alone. I had his younger son
for an apprentice and helper. You know
that after 15 years at Mystic, I still
dream about being back there in Salem
working for Fred.

Sorry about running on so long about
myself, but I had to establish my credentials
for passing on your evocation of Paul, his crew,
and his yard. It's great, it really is great.
I can see it, and see it all — smell it,
taste it, and feel it.

But I have been there, myself. Those who
haven't, as most have not, just how much
of it will they get, I wonder?

ployed in the Depression, food workers for the CIO, marriage and a
wife to support.

World War II brought the old-timers out of retirement, there were
jobs for everyone, it was a grand time to learn, and for almost 30 years
thereafter I worked on fine yachts, the last 20 before I came to Mystic
Seaport 15 years ago, at Fred Dion's yard in Salem, Massachusetts.

Fred was the same breed as Paul Luke, and ran the same kind of
yard, except that he specialized in servicing and repairing fine wooden
yachts, building very few. The same kind of joiner shop, the same sort
of crew, but no Baron. Fred was his own Baron. Fred and I got along
fine. Would give me a job and leave me alone. I had his younger son for

4

of course—there is much else in the Journal — solid, searching, intriguing, ~~thoughtful~~ thoughtful stuff, and things to argue over, too. I don't think you have the full Maine picture.

By the way, I have a copy of *Let Us Now Praise Famous Men*. Got it when it was first published many years ago. Things haven't changed much on the whole — for the worst if anything. Definitely for the worst on the world scale. Profligate waste, over-population, pollution, the atom, have brought humankind to the brink. At last we have the capability in our hands to destroy ourselves, and are likely to do so. But why do I write this? You know it as well as I do.

Hope you find a publisher. You write well, and it reads well. Ought to be in print.

I am sending this letter before I mail back your MS in case you may have changed your address. or something.

Best regards,

John Gardner

an apprentice and helper. You know that after 15 years at Mystic, I still dream about being back there in Salem working for Fred.

Sorry about running on so long about myself, but I had to establish my credentials for passing on your evocation of Paul, his crew, and his yard. It's great, it really is great. I can see it, and see it all—smell it, taste it, and feel it.

But I have been there, myself. Those who haven't, as most have not, just how much of it will they get, I wonder?

Of course there is much else in the Journal—solid, searching, intriguing, thoughtful stuff, and things to argue over, too. I don't think you have the full Maine picture.

By the way I have a copy of <u>Let</u> <u>Us</u> <u>Now</u> <u>Praise</u> <u>Famous</u> <u>Men</u>. Got it when it was first published many years ago. Things haven't changed much on the whole—for the worst if anything. Definitely for the worst on the world scale. Profligate waste, over-population, pollution, the atom have brought humankind to the brink. At last we have the capability in our hands to destroy ourselves, and are likely to do so. But why do I write this? You know it as well as I do.

Hope you find a publisher. You write well, and it reads well. Ought to be in print.

I am sending this letter before I mail back your Ms in case you may have changed your address, or something.

Best regards,
John Gardner

Ↄ   ↄ

Lastly a quote from John, WoodenBoat #40, page 40, May/June 1981: "John Gardner In His Own Words," an interview by Peter Spectre, to whom many thanks.

[With the advent of gasoline engines in the early 1900s] "everything changed, the old boatbuilders were no longer needed, they died off, and boatbuilding to the standards of the 19th century died with them. Such boatbuilding had never been recorded, as it had been carried on by rule-of-thumb methods. It was almost an illiterate trade until fairly recently. So with the advent of the gasoline engine, plus many other changes in American life brought on by the automobile, the bicycle, and the canvas canoe, we came to the end of an era."

Ↄ   ↄ

"John Gardner's work has engaged and inspired more individuals connected with traditional small craft than will ever be counted."

—*WoodenBoat* magazine

John Holt Willey's first formal writing was a poem for a high school English class, published in *Young America Sings*. Since then he has been a farmhand, janitor, jackhammer operator, U.S. Marine, choir member (bass), sailor, private investigator (San Francisco, sans glamour), electrician, boatbuilder, cabinetmaker, mason, and long served on the board of his beloved Good Will-Hinckley in Maine. Most of John's heroes are men and women who build things, but include Yeats, Frost, Millay, Carroll, and Will himself as evidenced in Chapter 4. In Maine coastal waters, he paddles an eighteen-foot sea kayak he built and launched in 1997. The author lives in central Maine near where he was born.